Break Through Fear
YOUR SPIRITUAL BUTT KICK

By

Landria Onkka

Dedication

I dedicate this book to my amazing and loyal followers, some of whom have listened to my teachings for years. Your support, outreach and love make the long hours of coaching, writing and shooting content worth it. You inspire me and are the catalyst for the beautiful planetary transformation that is taking place. I love you! Thank you for your love that you express to me daily. You have blessed my life and surely raise the frequency of the planet, one light being at a time!

Contents

EVERYTHING IS ONE THING 'HAPPENING.'

TIME DOES NOT EXIST.

'EVERYTHING' SEEN AND UNSEEN IS INTELLIGENT ENERGY, ONE FIELD, EVER EXPANDING, CREATING, EVOLVING, TRANSFORMING, EXPLORING ALL THAT IS POSSIBLE, WHICH IS UNLIMITED.

THIS 'EVERYTHING' IS ONE THING WITH NO BOUNDARIES FROM INFINITE NOTHINGNESS TO ALL KNOWING. IT IS BOTH CONSCIOUSNESS AND UNCONSCIOUSNESS. IT IS LIGHT AND DARKNESS AND EVERYTHING IN BETWEEN. IT IS PURITY AND ILLUSION POSING AS THE OPPOSITE OF THAT OF WHICH IT IS.

YOU, THE HUMAN, ARE AN EXPRESSION OF THE 'ONE' ENERGY. EVERYTHING IS BY CHOICE BECAUSE EVERYTHING AND NOTHING IS DIRECTED BY THE CREATOR WHICH IS ALL THINGS. BY CHOICE, WE FORGOT THIS AND CHOSE IGNORANCE.

YOU ARE THE 'EVERYTHING' THAT IS INTELLIGENCE EXPLORING SEPARATISM AND INDIVIDUALISM, IGNORANCE AND REDEMPTION. YOU ARE THE POWER THAT CREATES AND THE CREATED. YOU ARE THAT WHICH YOU BELIEVE IS THE 'OTHER.'

EVERYTHING THAT EXISTS IN EVERY DIMENSION AND EVERY TIME IS ONE 'NOW.'

TIME AS WE KNOW IT DOES NOT EXIST. IT IS AN ILLUSION THAT ALLOWS US TO EXPERIENCE A PAST WITH CHOICES THAT RESULT IN PRESENT RESULTS, AND PRESENT CHOICES THAT RESULT IN FUTURE RESULTS. CAUSE AND EFFECT IS HOW WE KNOW AND GAUGE OUR SPIRITUAL EVOLUTION. WE ARE CREATORS OF OUR OWN ILLUSIONS.

YOU HAVE BEEN AND WILL CONTINUE TO BE UNENDING EXPRESSIONS OF THE 'ONE' THAT IS BEYOND HUMAN COMPREHENSION. ALL IS AN ILLUSION CREATED BY THE ONE. CREATED BY YOU.

YOU ARE THE ENERGY THAT FLOWS THROUGH EVERYTHING. YOU ARE NOT SEPARATE FROM ANYTHING YOU SEE AND DO NOT SEE.

EVERYTHING IS IN CONSTANT AWARENESS OF ITSELF IN ITS ENDLESS FORMS AND AFFECTED BY THE ACTIONS OF EACH EXPRESSION.

HUMANS CANNOT UNDERSTAND THE GRAND LAWS OF THE UNIVERSE AND BEYOND. WE ARE THE CREATION THAT CHOSE TO NOT KNOW. IT IS PART OF OUR EXPERIENCE.

THERE IS NO REAL CHAOS BECAUSE EVEN CHAOS IS INTELLIGENTLY ORGANIZED. SOURCE IS ALL INTELLIGENCE.

OUR DENSITY KEEPS US IN PERCEIVED LIMITATIONS IN ORDER TO EXPERIENCE BEING HUMAN AND TO KNOW THE CONTRAST OF WHAT WE ARE.

DEATH AS WE KNOW IT, DOES NOT EXIST. NOTHING TRULY ENDS EXCEPT IN AN ILLUSION TO KNOW 'ENDINGS.'

THE 'ONE' IS AND WILL ALWAYS BE.

YOU HOLD THIS POWER. YOU ARE THIS POWER.

WHAT ARE YOU WAITING FOR?

YOU ARE MAGIC

"Life is difficult. This is a great truth, one of the greatest truths. It is a great truth because once we truly see this truth, we transcend it. Once we truly know that life is difficult - once we truly understand and accept it - then life is no longer difficult." The Road Less Traveled

Well, this isn't exactly so true is it? No matter what spiritual state of awakening you may be in, chances are pretty good that life is still difficult. It is designed to be that way.

EVERYTHING IS ONE THING 'HAPPENING'
TIME DOES NOT EXIST

This the information I received while in a super awakened state that pretty much says it all. But, what does it mean? There is nothing separate, therefore, everything is one thing. Time does not exist, which means that all 'things' and events exist at once, including what we refer to as past and future. You and I are not 'happening' as individuals but functioning as the illusion of that. We are One energy. Because of our unconscious state that does not recognize this, we oppose one another and battle for our individual needs. This creates disharmony which is part of the duality of the universe. It is intentional.

Things on planet Earth are getting serious but this is no surprise. We have functioned as self-serving beings unaware of our origins, the essence of what we are, or the power we wield. This is by design. We have focused on our seemingly three-dimensional world and placed its material goods and how they can serve us above all else because we operate from limitations and endings. We believe the illusion that we created and deny the magic that we hold to transform it. The illusion is the game of discovery. It is the unconscious state of the One finding its way back to consciousness in order to know itself. To be human is to play the game of unconsciousness.

We look into the sky, aware that we are floating in black space with no clue as to what is truly 'out there' with no real appreciation of its grandeur. What suspends us in the nothingness and why? How does it all work? What is it and what is beyond it? We cannot comprehend this vast magnificence, so our focus turns to our limited needs not recognizing that the intelligence that flows through all is always at our beck and call and that we are that very intelligence. Despite our view of that vast, mysterious and infinite space, we continue to believe in limitations. What are we? Why are we here and what is the purpose of anything? The vast void that we are floating in is too frightening for us. Our dense condition prompts us to feel small and insignificant instead of vast and powerful. This is because we believe it is separate from us just as separate as we see one another. Humans are threatened by what they do not understand.

We are participating in the most challenging hologram in the universe; the ultimate virtual game. Will we pull out of density and return to singularity? Will we come to terms with our power? We are now experiencing the tipping point of our destructive actions as a species and are at a nexus point when decisions must be made in order to determine how this game evolves.

It is time for a spiritual butt kick, an awakening to what we are, to take responsibility for all that is, has been, will be, and most of all what 'can be.' There is no more time or tolerance for finger pointing. Finger pointing is at the root of our planetary struggles and it is time to recognize that what is happening on our planet was and is a result of OUR beliefs, OUR thoughts, OUR actions and OUR choices. Yes, that includes you. You are a creator not only when you consciously place your attention on a desire, but at every moment. There is no 'outside source' or middle man that determines your worth or if you deserve abundance, health and happiness. That decisionmaker, that creator that grants such things is the person you see in the mirror every day.

You may be uncomfortable with some of the things I will present and that is okay. Change is uncomfortable and accepting that we wield unlimited power can be overwhelming. It places full responsibility on us, but it also empowers you to change any situation in your life. Used in the frequency of love and peace, it can transform our world into a state of heaven. This does not take time. It is possible now simply by choice. Everyone has that choice.

Humans have been seeking answers to the big 'why' for centuries. No answer can ever satisfy simply because humans cannot comprehend the magnitude of the truth. Now, more than ever, we are willing to break away from traditional beliefs and our programming to find answers that ultimately can never be understood. Mind blowing discoveries in quantum mechanics have demonstrated the connection of all things and opened the door to realities never thought possible. What else is 'out there' that will reveal that we are not what we thought we were? What are we actually capable of, that we have not begun to tap into? We are just beginning to openly discuss expansive subjects without fear of harm or shaming, although there are those in professional positions who continue to be stifled and shunned. Fortunately, more are speaking out regardless of the repercussions. It is time to make the impossible possible.

Change is a constant, but get ready because there are even BIGGER changes to come. The tipping point, which we will cover in detail, is here and the effects of humanity's actions are unfolding in an accelerated manner. From our health to the planet's health, how we handle abundance and one another, expect to see the 'karmic' repercussions of it all. As unpleasant as it sounds, pain is the best motivator for positive change. Pain has always been our motivator and in typical human form, as a result of our ongoing destructive behavior, we find ourselves faced with critical life and planetary decisions that can no longer be avoided. What we have dished out has manifested for all to experience because all choices affect the collective. Disregard for others and the planet was a message received and demonstrated in the material world. Will we find the answers to our dilemma that will take us out of conflict and destruction and into a state of peace? We are exhausted. Is that how you feel? Do you feel that it is time to end suffering for yourself and others? We have explored this dense condition for long enough and experienced the unending cycle of pain it has inflicted on our species. It is not our essence. We can do better. It only requires one decision by you.

It is time to speak up and shout from the rooftops that we are ready to do what it takes to align with what is best and highest for all humans, all life forms and this amazing planet that we claim as our home. Conformity is obsolete. It has not served us well. Conforming is what has kept us in a perpetual state of unhappiness. Fear is at the root of this. We fear pain, loss, and the end of our existence. We fear one another because we live in separation. I am here along with many others at this moment in time, to deliver a spiritual butt kick because each one of us is powerful beyond our imagination. It is time to use our powers for healing, abundance, joy and miracles. There is no outside source we must ask for these things. The 'ask' we refer to is simply our own directive through thoughts fueled by our beliefs. However, fear has been at the foundation of our beliefs. You may think you believe one thing, but behind it may lie fear. Fear cancels out expansion and the manifestation of what you desire never quite materializes. Instead you find that the same things you don't desire appear. It knows what you believe. It knows what you know. You and it are one.

I liken us to a power source that has been placed in the basement for centuries, ready at any time to be activated, covered in dust and ignored. Like the beggar in tattered robes whose pockets are filled with jewels, never reaching into them, we ignore our treasures and thus continue to struggle. The answers to our problems are not to be found. They are here, right now, in plain sight. They are within you and the essence of everything. They always have been. We need only recognize them.

Our greatest discovery is that there are no problems. How can there be when we are the director of our own story and the very creators of them? Therefore, our problems must be choices. But why? Everything serves a divine purpose of knowledge. We are collectors of experiences and adventures, no matter what that includes. Problems are simply exploration of that which the One is curious to know. No species knows or creates problems better than humans.

Being human is unique. We have a body that has needs, and experience the unpleasant results when they are not met. We fight and compete for resources to keep it satisfied and alive even though we are fully aware that no one can maintain 'life' as we know it here. We find honor in dying for the cause of life which in turn will also expire. What is it we are actually trying to keep 'alive?' That which is truly alive is the eternal power that animates all of it which need not be 'fought for' or protected. It is difficult for humans to imagine that they hold the power of the universe within them that transcends anything that could possibly threaten it. We mourn death because we believe it is an ending even though it is equal to birth – a glorious transition.

I am not here to help you because you don't need help. I only hope to be a guide whom can light the way, because you are equally as powerful and capable as any person on the planet now or who has ever existed. I am here to remind you of who and what you are. Whether it is through advanced discoveries in science revealing our mysterious quantum powers or your own mind-blowing experiences, we are recognizing that we indeed are much greater than imagined. We shall explore this power and how you can tap into it starting today.

It is time for us to place others first in every aspect. Our final planetary outcome depends on it because like your human body, all parts must work together in order to maintain health. "What you do to the least of us, you do to me," are the words of Christ. What did he mean by this? The 'other' is you and that judgement, blame, greed or criticism you impose on others, you do to yourself and all of us. Separation and opposition are at the root of our pain and planetary demise. There is a simple solution to this conflict, yet the ego refuses to let go of its focus on self-service and gratification. It is used to being in control. It believes that anything not directly feeding its needs and interests is ultimately expendable. It seeks survival because it believes in endings. This is the directive that has placed us in a position of potential extinction. What we do to the 'other' we do to ourselves. How have you treated 'the other?'

Will we choose awakening or destruction? There is another aspect to this that may instill hope in you. While we are part of a collective future that changes at every moment through our choices, we are also privileged to experience individual outcomes. There is no one reality that all humans experience. The collective is the shared illusion of planet earth and is the 'everything' that extends to all other illusions. The collective is an energy field of which we contribute individual frequencies. We each participate in chosen realities yet remain connected. My decision affects you, because we share a collective experience. This gets a little tricky and no person can fully know the magic of the cosmos and its rules, but I assure you that no matter what is to come, you do not have to experience the worst of it. You have the ability to shift into what many refer to as the 'new earth.' There is a journey each must take in order to get there. We agreed to play out our roles as dense humans to earn such a state of being. All is a brilliant adventure designed just for you, by you and a collective, and is an amazing story that unfolds at every moment. What one person may struggle with, could be your shining moment and passage to awakening and euphoria. Your new earth exists right now despite what you witness happening around you because reality is not the 3-D world you see. It is what you do not see, and everyone is allowed passage to that knowledge.

So, with your contribution to the collective along with directing your own experience, I shall be blunt. It is time to stop blaming the world and one another, and take responsibility for everything undesirable that appears in our lives including the collective and that 'other' person you blame for your woes. It isn't the government, your parents, society, your spouse, or the bully who tortured you as a kid that is the problem. There are no problems. There are only experiences designed by you, played out with other willing participants for the purpose of growth and contrast. Your free will choice is always in action. It is time to recognize these challenges as the reason we came here and not see them as events to be avoided or opposed.

Unfortunately, centuries of pain have not taught us much. We continue to listen to that dense and self-serving energy field called the 'ego' that consistently produces conflict with others and within ourselves. As a species, we claim that we hate living this way, yet we continue to operate in the same destructive manner that can lead us to self-annihilation. We are the creators of 'that way' that we live. No one imposes that upon us. We fund research to find cures for cancer and eat chemical laden foods while in the waiting room before a chemo treatment. We rally for clean water and then fertilize our lawns with deadly sprays. The breast milk of American women is saturated with plastic from our polluted waters and those mothers bathe their babies in that same toxic water, and feed them poison preservative laden baby foods. We ask why God would allow starvation when we are totally capable of distributing the plentiful foods our planet produces.

While we are on the precipice of great change, a vast majority of humans have not progressed spiritually. This is about to be remedied. The accumulation of our planetary destructive energy and past self-serving actions has pushed us to a tipping point. We have help. Other energies have joined us to supply gateways to a higher way and to shine light. You must make a choice. No one can do that for you. 'Seek and you shall find' means that it takes a conscious effort to manifest that which you desire. You must choose through your own free will directive, to create. You hold that power. Currently, the majority manifest through their unconscious thoughts which are primarily of a negative nature. The density humans have created on this planet along with the new earth of peace exist simultaneously. Which will you choose? Don't worry. If you don't make it this time, you can always come back for another 'go' at it. My guess is that you would prefer to avoid that option. So, let's get it right this time, shall we?

The material world is pretty convincing and consumes our attention, making what lies beyond it unimportant and incomprehensible. The unseen power, that space between each material item, is uncomfortable turf because we associate primarily with that which we can see and touch. We are discovering that the unseen is not dead space after all, but in fact intelligence that is responsible for our visible world and more powerful than we can know. That nothingness is the source of that which we cling to and call reality. How can that be? Is it acting independently? Is it something to fear? Does it have a separate agenda? All of these questions are easily answered although never fully understood. We will explore all of them.

Then there is the whole subject of awakening or "enlightenment" that is always popular when things aren't going well for us. We are told that it is a desirable state of euphoria that eludes most. We have preconceived ideas about what it is and clueless as to how to obtain it simply because we use human logic to understand something no human can. It is like being told what chocolate tastes like if you've never tasted it, or describing a color never seen. Awakening is of great interest because it promises an escape from the pain of the world, but usually sought only when everything in life fails. Pain is the great motivator because when the ego is satisfied, it has no reason to pursue anything else. Only awakening provides an everlasting escape from struggle, not reliant on the material world that can never fulfill us. The challenge is 'how to achieve it?' Humans think in density and spend their time seeking it as if working toward a higher position in a corporation. They believe it arrives with practices and rituals, specific lifestyle changes, giving up the material world, or isolation. It is none of these things. It is not something to obtain. It is already the essence of you. It is the shedding of the illusion of everything else that reveals the true you, the awakened source. You were always carrying the jewels in your pocket. Simply reach in.

When the world is running smoothly on the ego's terms, awakening becomes a future goal if one at all. There is even less incentive to awaken as we have been told a sacrifice of riches is required to be 'spiritual.' We believe that we may have to give up luxuries, indulgences, and spend hours meditating. Imagine not needing to compete, or win. It seems like awakening is no fun at all. These 'sacrifices' go against the motive of the ego to acquire all that feeds its needs and importance. Enlightenment becomes something to pursue before we die when we have exhausted all of our material desires and want to assure our place in heaven.

15

Until that time, why would we want to pursue something that is not only incomprehensible but seems to offer so little? The ego promises more, so we believe. It offers happiness through tangible material goods and emotional highs. Thus, the world continues on in its quest to consume what it sees.

There is hope. Great changes are taking place from the individual experience to the collective, revealing great new discoveries about what we are and what we are capable of. All of this is fueled by the pain we have created that is now reflected throughout our entire planet. This pain is the direct result of the ego and like the suffering individual who sees no other options, an entire planet looks to awaken, to escape and repair the damages inflicted on our home. The threat of total destruction has motivated us. Humanity is beginning to trust that unknown realm, because the material world as we know it no longer offers satisfactory solutions. We are beginning to understand that we created our material world and all of the repercussions of our actions. Basically, we have trashed it and are living in our own toilet. These 'problems' that we see around us are not happening 'to us' but are created 'by us.' This is good news because if we are the creators, we can change everything.

There are those that believe that the world is happening 'to us,' that we are trapped on a 'prison planet' and our primary focus is survival. They play the role of victims with a belief that nothing painful holds purpose and that their choices have little impact beyond their immediate reality. This victim mentality creates anger, despair and anxiety because it rests on the belief that they are not manifesting their own reality. After all, if we are so powerful, why would we choose anything that causes pain? If we come from bliss, what would be the point in leaving it? The ego rejects any circumstance that does not produce satisfaction through the material world. Therefore, its mission is to seek and obtain more and more, often at the expense of others.

Like the butterfly that flaps its wings that slowly builds up to a storm, so YOU impact our planet from your thoughts to your actions. There is nothing that you do or do not do that goes without causing universal change. Our choices are the power we hold in the form of free will. These choices are always in action and interacting with other choices. When you grasp the power of the One individual that is the One of everything, you can then understand the importance of your decisions and how far reaching they are. When you make higher choices (service to others), I assure you that no matter what takes place on our planet, your great awakening is assured. By serving the whole, you will reap amazing results despite what plays out. You then become the butterfly that emerges from the cocoon, flaps its wings that causes the eventual hurricane.

What is this great transformation, the Great Awakening that many believe will take us to an era of peace? Is it a realization that we have no other choice than to get our act together or perish? Perhaps it is the planetary 'dark night of the soul' that is pushing us to claw our way back to harmony. Is awakening simply the ego protecting its own interests by trying everything that can save its own world? Only the ego believes that awakening includes separation of itself from 'them' and 'us,' 'right' and 'wrong.' A movement of the righteous to battle evil is further separation into darkness and is in no way part of the awakening. The One is the light and the dark. Embracing it equally is the only path to consciousness. True awakening goes beyond names or labels, right or wrong, good or bad, or fighting for anything. It is knowing beyond that which can be explained.

The great awakening is simply to know that everything is self-created, equally powerful, connected and equally loved. It is service to others and compassion for all. No one gets left behind. That is impossible because that which is darkness is connected to that which is light. No human can 'leave' behind that which is itself. There is no alien space craft that will whisk away the good people and leave the others behind to suffer. Nothing comes to an end. It simply transforms. Awakening is the conscious state that we are the everything and nothing, the light and the illusion, the power that creates it all and the player who cries out for mercy.

As more realize Oneness, the collective will experience a state of peace and love that we have never known in human form. That which you once judged and despised will light up when you love it without conditions because it is you. And you, like it, desire love. Love is the only transformational gateway into awakening. It is our essence. Unconditional love is all that is required.

Awakening is a state of euphoria that you can experience while standing next to someone who only sees despair and pain on the planet. It does not require others to awaken. It recognizes the light in the other and understands that those we despise the most are our greatest teachers. The great awakening is the era wherein humans become the best of their material existence because they have recognized their true essence. It is then that we may exhibit miraculous feats that have always been ours to use simply because we 'know' that we hold such power. We are awakening to the fact that we are the One Force that flows through and creates everything, that is everything.

Awakening is the knowing that we are the divine experiencing unconsciousness in the form of the dense human.

Now is the moment of critical choice. We are experiencing the repercussions of what we have been as a species, how we have treated one another and our planet, and we are here to change it all. Why? Because that is the game. We as an expansive energy field, are always looking to experience a new adventure and within it, progress. Progress is the 'knowing' of contrast and the teachings that present opportunities to make higher choices. And yes, that includes you, because you are the centuries of personalities that brought us to this place. No one person can say that they did not contribute to our current state because we are all One, existing in all space and beyond time. There is no getting around this. When you accept this responsibility, your world will shift in a most powerful, profound way. Taking responsibility will set you free from the constraints you have lived under. Responsibility and acceptance together will empower you in ways you have never known.

Herein comes the true challenge that you signed up for. If we want to create that which we claim we desire, a world of peace, health and abundance, we must be prepared to work through this 'effect' from the 'cause' of our past actions and those before us. The planetary crises are a direct reflection of our disregard for all things outside of our personal interests. It is that simple. We have not respected life on all levels, and it is handing us back all that we have given it, unleashing the darkness that we created with a fury. Reparations are in order which are taking place as our communities unite.

While all things are possible, we must deal with the results of self-serving manifestations which may be unpleasant until we 'unwind' it all. Along with that unpleasant effect is also the excitement and exhilaration of knowing that we are transitioning into something amazing. Our free will that brought every human here to participate in this planetary shift makes each of us quite bold and, frankly, quite brave. No matter how discouraged or defeated you may feel, I promise you that you ARE up for the challenge. Your presence here is not a random act nor an accident. There is no chaos in the universe except that which we choose, but even that is organized. Something beautiful is transpiring and you signed up for it. So, brush yourself off and get out there. Amazing events and results await you.

To go from material desires, to recognizing that we are the essence of the universal One and all powerful is a big leap, but it is possible, and it is happening. This transformation is not achieved through the thinking mind but a state of being that naturally shifts you into a totally new dimension. Despite the pain we witness all around us, positive change is taking place. If you are not experiencing a world that is heading toward that change, then perhaps it is time to shift your reality by shifting your beliefs and thus your actions. You will then be redirected toward and contribute to this positive change and your world will transform simply because you see it that way. You cannot tune into a rock and roll radio station and hear classical music. Each must align with the frequency that they desire to live. I liken it to leaving the basement, getting on the elevator and going up to the penthouse. The view is quite different and amazing from there. You may have spent your entire life in that basement, only knowing darkness while all the time that penthouse always existed in the very same mansion. In darkness it is difficult to see the doors or know that there is light outside of that space. Each floor represents the frequency you align with and only you are pushing the buttons on that elevator. You are in control. I will show you that it IS that simple if you master the steps I present.

An understanding is required to activate the powerful source of which we are, not just individually, but as One unstoppable, perfect light that flows through all things. From there we, as role playing humans, may connect to what lies within and beyond the illusionary body. This is The Great Awakening, the path to the new earth. This new earth is not a place we 'go to,' but a recognition that we are already perfect and can simply shift into that perfection. It is a state of being that exists for all of us; another dimension right here on planet earth. It is not something to find, but something to recognize, to awaken to. With contrast comes deep understanding of what love truly is. That love becomes even more powerful when we experience what it is like to know the lack of it. Lack, of course, is an illusion but a powerful one. Transitioning from an unconscious state into light while still inhabiting the human body makes the experience that much more impactful and remarkable.

Struggle, pain and fear is uniquely fabricated for and by humans. It is the ultimate experience; the ultimate training ground; the ultimate reveal. To discover our perfection through the myriad of games that disguise it is the ultimate goal of the game. To live in great density and pain only to recognize that we always were perfect is our big 'ah ha' moment. Once we realize that we are and always were the source of pain in order to know our perfection, we can end it. Struggle is simply non-acceptance. It is the battle of the ego and separation of all things. Struggle is when we find no purpose in our pain. We deny it, battle it, and try to change the circumstances that created it instead of examining the reason it appeared in the first place. This can end in an instance, but it takes a 'rewiring' of sorts to overcome the conditioning of the human mind. Acceptance is required in order to transition into peace. I do not refer to the acceptance of destruction but of the human condition and its purpose in the bigger scheme of the universe.

Fear does not exist in the new earth because enlightened beings do not facilitate actions that prompt fear. The ego has dissolved and service to others creates a condition of unity, joy and expansion. In this dimension, challenges continue but are received as opportunities for growth. It is impossible for fear to exist on that plane because fear is not on the same frequency as love. They exist on separate floors in the mansion and you have to get on the elevator and push the button to get to the penthouse. The trick is that the elevator is powered by your personal frequency that will take you to the floor of which you resonate. It is bright and beautiful in the penthouse. There, all of your needs and desires are met! No two journeys or pathways to gain access are the same. This is the uniqueness of every human. There is no one 'way' to awaken. In fact, there is nothing to 'get to' or achieve. You already are that which you seek. Awakening is to know this and release everything else. It is the 'everything else' that is the illusion, serving an amazing purpose. We leave the stories, the separation and illusions on the lower floors, stripping them away as we make our way to the penthouse.

Despite all of the indications that we hold the power of great change, we continue to cling to fear. 'Letting go' has not been as easy as anticipated. Knowing the potential rewards, why on Earth (literally) would we find releasing fear so damned difficult? It has become so 'real' and tangible to us that we can't imagine living without it. We believe that it is something that happens to us and not that which we alone create. It has become an addiction and a barrier to manifesting miracles. We are so used to fear and struggle that when presented with peace, we continue to gravitate toward creating more pain. Pain, we know. Peace, well that is a different feeling and to humans can be quite boring.

The opposite of fear is faith. Humans don't like to hand control over to an intangible power that has no guarantees. Faith means that we may have to endure discomfort while we hang onto that which promises something higher and not necessarily in our lifetime. Faith is unknown and 'out there' that we believe requires 'giving up' things we value. Fear is familiar and it represents our rejection of all that is bad or wrong, meaningless and painful. How could we possibly believe that anything painful holds any positive purpose for us? Fear makes more sense. Handing control over to what we believe is a separate unknown decisionmaker creates great discomfort. Yes, fear is much more under our control. Faith is not, or so we believe.

More humans are fed up with living unfulfilled lives despite material gain. Our glimpse of quantum powers is beginning to hold promise of our ability to affect great change. So, if we have had enough of suffering, why don't we just simply end it? After all, if we are the source of its creation, then we are also the source of its potential demise. Most don't know where to begin. Our challenge is that we don't believe it. The ego believes that there is something or someone else that is at the root of our problems. We know separation quite well. It is always an outside source that is the problem – the government, our parents, our boss, big money, and even a God that decides what we do and do not deserve. We are told that to think of ourselves as an equal source of this power is blasphemous and punishable in the afterlife. This is part of the matrix conditioning that is strong within our energy field on this planet. This is the control that we are continually lured into through addictive fear tactics by others who would have us believe we are powerless. This is demonstrated through the small percentage of people who control the majority of material wealth and power.

There is that whole timing issue too. Not everyone is ready and willing to let go and let God. Many still have adventures and teachings that they scheduled to experience. Regardless of our limited time here, we always think that there is more of it and that something will happen that will change everything for our planet. We believe that some higher power is going to come down and save us regardless of our behavior. Humans have been waiting for that 'big event' and constantly look to the future as the answer. The answer to our salvation exists right now. It is the choice that you make today. It is not him or her or them that stands in the way. There is only you that changes your life, and thus the universe and beyond.

It is a fact that humans gravitate to that which is 'familiar' even if it is destructive. The ego doesn't like change because unknown turf equates to loss of control. The ego does not know what to do with peace, unconditional giving, love and compassion. It has no use for it unless it is receiving something valuable from it all. Peace

23

requires collective cooperation which it does not know. Separation is its expertise. After all, what would the ego gain from that except for accolades? Even giving is motivated by personal attention, self-satisfaction and adoration. The ego will even 'fight' for peace and battle evil, not believing that any act of hate or destruction is the very evil it seeks to eliminate.

When the ego isn't busy grabbing satisfaction through more 'stuff', it will often demean others with the goal of elevating itself. There is that judgement thing that it loves to dish out that makes others wrong and the root of our problems. It loves to be the master of struggle because it is good at creating and living with it. Pain and struggle create and reinforce the game that it knows, claims to avoid, but unconsciously perpetuates. The ego has a fascination with struggle and contrast. It is an addiction. We will explore the reasons for this further.

The ego wants the world to revolve around its beliefs and desires. It loves control and can be disguised in a 'shy' façade, a caring or even spiritual one. This is not planned deception but a genuine belief that what the ego believes is truth. This is unconsciousness. Any upheavals and changes that push the ego's desire further away are perceived as negative and unwanted. It finds no value in delays. So, the ego battles them, spiraling downward and clinging to outside answers from other sources, often in desperation. Other egos take advantage of this and preach more fear, for the benefit of their own agendas, offering satisfaction to other egos with self-serving intentions. And, so history repeats itself.

It appears that we have not learned a damned thing but despite it all, there is a strong movement made up of small numbers powerful enough to affect great change. Those not tuned in, will not be aware of it. This is because the new earth is not one defined place, event, or state of being for everyone. It is a personal choice that allows each of us to exist in our own realities. This is the discovery that needs no proof of 'how' it all works, but is proof in results that are taking place all over this planet. Is it happening for you? If not, keep reading.

Let us consider the conditioning that has kept us in this cycle of pain. Why is peace and awakening versus pain and destruction such a big decision to make? Isn't peace versus pain a 'no brainer?' We may say "Of course," but our actions certainly don't reflect that statement. Enlightenment is considered a sacrifice of so many things that we believe are important, including abundance. We are told that enlightened beings are to be pious and live an austere life. This is the ego's conditioning that believes that it will be held back from its material comforts. Egos that understand their manifesting powers do not want higher frequency beings to be in charge. After all, enlightened humans would share and 'give.' A world of giving distributes wealth. Miracles would be every day occurrences. Egos use their powers for control so that they can get more, more, more of everything. If others are 'giving,' it certainly threatens the belief of egos that resources are limited. It messes up their whole plan of dominance and greed.

Who in their right mind would seek enlightenment when it means giving up all that the ego believes is happiness? Therefore, enlightenment remains an obscure place that we hesitate to explore unless pushed to extremes. It is only too often when all else has not satisfied that we seek that last resort. When we arrive at that moment, the ego is usually still in operation trying to save itself. It 'wants' a solution to its worldly pain and embarks on a journey to find it. Yet the key to enlightenment is not to find it, but to let go and allow it. No sacrifice of abundance is required. When one comes into the understanding of his or her true essence, all riches, joy, and happiness appear without even a thought. The material world is yours, always has been, and is always being created by you. It is not an outside source that makes it happen, but is your manifestation to produce. Your requests are never threatened because all things exist at every moment and are accessible to all. Enlightenment opens the door to abundance, health, and happiness because it knows no barriers like the ones that ego creates. Ironically, the enlightened being with access to all then no longer requires any 'thing' to be happy. This is the simple life that we often see. It is not a sacrifice, but a choice because the happiness that was once sought through the material world exists without it.

Humans believe that there is a checklist that can take them to enlightenment, seeking answers and secrets outside of themselves to achieve it. True to human form, we believe it is something 'out there' to obtain. Are these the right rituals? Are we saying the correct mantra? Have we purchased the right crystals or burned the right candles? Will this be the teacher that opens the gateway for us? We are clueless about this space of existence and operate in fear of what will happen to us should we miss the looming deadline of the end of the world. Like everything else that we desire, we chase it. The truth is that no one nor set of practices can give you enlightenment. It is already yours. It is everything else that is false. Enlightenment is the essence of you and simply awaits to be discovered. Unwrap the illusion and you will reveal it.

Humans constantly see the world as the problem that holds them back from their material and relationship goals. They believe that others are separate and that evil itself is an independent force that battles for our souls. That is a load of crap, of course, unless you believe it. Then it would be totally true for you. Belief makes it so. Most of the world believes the crap and thus are swimming in their own dirty toilets. Herein is how we create our individual realities and outcomes. Are you catching on? You are creating everything for YOU. You and you alone are directing your reality, your challenges, and your triumphs. Only YOU allow awakening. Arguing with any other human about reality is fruitless because everyone is right. If there was one truth, one right and one wrong, then free will could not be in operation.

It is time for us to get off of our butts and take responsibility for the struggle and suffering we have inflicted on this beautiful planet and one another. It is all about YOU because you are everything and everyone. I am not speaking of you the human but YOU the One Source. YOU are not only the recipient of your abuse but also that person who abused you. You are the wino on the street, the saint, the murderer and the unseen. YOU are everything you inflict, that you give and that you receive. It is you, and it is me. There is no line between the energy of each of us, the plant, the rock, the butterfly. It is One.

What about that all-pervasive emotion we name fear? It is the most powerful emotion that rules humanity. Fear is at the root of all suffering. It is the belief that nothing painful or challenging holds value and so we battle it through denial and rejection. We then amplify the fear, waking up at 3 am envisioning the worst-case scenario with an even deeper dread. We have all been there and done that, and it is time to move onto a better use of our creative powers.

We are in charge of everything that has taken place, and WE are in charge of everything that happens from the present moment onward. Fear creates balance within the matrix because it offers insights into possibilities and motivates change. Only when it is believed to be ultimate truth without choice does it create destructive domination.

Despite being a part of One energy contributing to the collective, your story is not everyone's story. Your ending does not have to be another's no matter what the odds or past outcomes have demonstrated under certain circumstances. Fear is an unmistakable central point of the human experience and can be used in the most positive and powerful manner. You can use your fears to take action toward positive change which in turn changes the algorithms within the matrix. Fear can be the story you imagine that never has to take place if you use it to motivate you. The odds change, and the beggar becomes the millionaire. The underdog wins the gold medal. All things then truly become possible because fear no longer controls you but drives you to different results. Fear is the emotion that brings duality into our hologram, that provides the balance of challenges and triumphs.

Nothing goes unnoticed. From a belief to a thought to an action and even inaction, there are direct effects on the universe. This is unavoidable. As everything is One, it makes sense that every 'thing,' every expression, effects the whole. It is instantaneous with no time delay. Like the cut on your finger that is connected to and felt by your hand, that is part of your limb, and your body, everything that you do affects all energy in all spaces. We can change anything because we are everything. We are the darkness and the light. Light, however, is our foundation and anything that emanates from that is an exploration of its contrast. It is all under our control. When we recognize this and release the fear-based beliefs that something outside of us is creating our pain, the illusion dissolves and we are off to play a new game. It will, preferably, be less challenging and painful! If we master this game, our next venture most certainly WILL be as these lessons are no longer needed.

Want to know the secret to the game? You have and are everything you need or desire. It exists within you right now and all probabilities await your directives. You must know this to win. Since the One, the Source of all is the singularity, which is of the highest frequency, everything else that manifests are illusions. Forgetting this allows us to know the illusion which challenges even the most enlightened beings. All that we explore becomes another layer of illusion over the foundation of the essence of you. You can continue to collect layers that dim your light, or you can peel them away. Awakening is not something that anyone must seek. To seek is simply to place a request, a directive, into the quantum field that always gives you exactly what you ask for. When you 'seek,' that which you desire is revealed to you and not 'brought' to you simply because it already resides within. Since you are all things, you only need direct your focus on that which you 'seek' to materialize it into your reality. This focus must be clear and a true belief that one envisions or 'knows' at which time it becomes 'real' for you within the holographic menu.

Thus, the game of life begins, and the teachings lead us back to euphoria. It is yours to claim at any time, but you may not be ready for it. You may, through choice, want to KNOW suffering, illness, anger, loneliness. After all, we do not know these feelings outside of our human bodies. We cannot know pain when we are in our natural state of light because they are different frequencies. Therefore, human density creates limitations for us. How amazing to know loss, despair and most of all fear. How even more amazing to overcome it all. THIS is what it is to be human. It is an experience like none other in the entire universe and possibly beyond.

It is time to stop finger pointing at 'the other.' There is no 'other.' There is only you, the 'I Am' of all illusion and the 'I Am' that creates it. You are the driving force behind all that transpires because nothing you experience can BE unless you willingly participate in it. YOU flow through that which you point at. It is time for the great awakening to this fact. It is time to end the excuses and the victimization because we hold and ARE the power of the universe, capable of anything. The movement toward this realization is happening with or without your participation, but all of it will affect you because you ARE also 'that out there.' Will you continue to experience pain and suffering or move into bliss and unconditional love? The new earth awaits and is happening now. You can be the facilitator of its glorious reveal. The choice is yours alone. To evolve is an amazing conclusion to the human experience. Regardless of your decision, know that you cannot escape this Earthly form and its story. You chose it. You're here. So why not make the best of it? I assure you that if you do, the 'best' is beyond human comprehension. Are you ready to embrace that?

ONE CONSCIOUSNESS

What we are has been a mystery since the beginning of human existence. Let me clarify that. What we are has been a mystery to humans. Other realms and higher beings have a clear knowing of this and if there was a sect of humans who had this answer, they certainly did not pass down the secret. Therefore, we continue to wonder why we are here, with no concrete proof of our origins or how long we have inhabited Earth. Any suggestions outside of our human religious teachings is rejected because to think otherwise is infused with fears of cataclysmic consequences and retribution. Our beliefs are riddled with limitations and fear.

We have a sense of something greater, yet most of humanity has discouraged the exploration of what that could be. Why? What is so frightening to us that we recoil from exploring unseen powers that we know could hold the answers to the universe? Why do humans choose limitations for themselves and impose them on others? What is it that we fear?

Oneness is a word that humans cannot comprehend because we live in a material world and its perceived individualism. We believe the material world. You and I are separate in our illusion and my physical view of that confirms it. After all, what else is there if not that which we can see and touch? Besides, you may not like me at all! So how could 'we' be one?

We value our individualism and protect it. We have no interest in anything that we do not understand that does not appear to serve our needs. Sure, quantum physics has demonstrated that there is an energy that flows through all things and that we affect these things with observation but what does that mean to the father juggling his work and family relationship, the single mother struggling to make ends meet, or the student stressing about her upcoming exams? Each see their and others actions translating into desirable or undesirable effects and that is all that matters. Do we have what we need? Are we getting what we desire? If we aren't satisfying our needs, then what else could be more important? Why do others seem to have it so easy while you or I struggle?

Why should we care about quantum physics and how does it relate to us? Science does not have the answers because science relies on material results and nothing is truly 'material.' It approaches answers with a closed mind that is unbending. Is light a wave or particle? It is both, yet scientists continue to seek one answer as truth. The unlimited creator is all things in all time. The material world is simply conscious intelligence appearing as form. You don't need science to prove anything to you. Break through fear, manifest miracles, and see what scientists say. They will most likely brush it off as a freak anomaly or coincidence. Science has not fully embraced that consciousness is one thing intelligently operational at all times. If we dared to open ourselves to that which is unknown, mystical and magical events would occur that would produce profound effects. We need no proof or explanation of how this is possible.

Let us get to the core of real power, the One Consciousness. What is the One Consciousness? It is the One power that pervades and is all things. This power is expansive, creative energy. It is intelligence beyond what science can know or ever prove. It is everything you see and do not see. This includes a rock, your table, water, a cloud, animals and all humans. It is also that 'space' that appears empty, dark energy and dark matter.

God is not only the power that created all, but is the power that animates it. In fact, everything is directed by intelligent directives whether conscious or unconscious. It is the power of no thing and every thing. That space that separates our material world is equally intelligent; the essence of God, Source, the One Consciousness. They are one in the same. That 'God' that we place in a separate space from us, above us, somewhere out in the cosmos is you. This must be so because nothing is separate. There is a statement that we are made in the image of God, but what does that mean? That image isn't a human, it's light. Everything is light, posing as 'something' through its expansive explorations. You are light. You are from light and light is the essence of all things, even the darkness that we see. Darkness is simply a different vibration of the one consciousness of all things that poses as unconsciousness at times. Humans are that demonstration.

THE UNCONSCIOUSNESS OF SOURCE

Perhaps you are not on board with the One Consciousness being 'all things' and all nothingness. After all, that is a pretty big idea for us earthlings to comprehend. How can 'something' that is 'everything' be 'nothing?' For just a moment, let us explore that idea with an open mind.

If we are the One intelligence exploring every probability conceivable, then one of those probabilities is 'unconsciousness.' Yes, unconsciousness. In other words, 'not knowing itself' is also a form of its exploration. We are that. As One Consciousness, expanding, exploring, and creating with no limits then it is no surprise that it created the state of not knowing itself. After all, it is Source and unlimited, so it is not surprising that it would create an unconscious form. The 'unconscious' mind of the Source is one of the extreme explorations of its unlimited powers and we are the creation of 'not knowing.' We are the Creator experiencing the unconscious mind; the creation that has no recollection of what it is. Does this shock you or does this somehow make perfect sense? Perhaps this is the 'never being comfortable' feeling that you may have experienced most or all of your life. We exist with other humans, those just like us sharing the same home, yet it is this co-habitation that feels so uncomfortable. We simply don't seem to like one another or get along very well. This is because we are playing a role of separation. We are always aware that we are 'that' while playing 'this.' In other words, as all things, we carry the knowing that we are unlimited source even as we play the role of the limited human. It is impossible to disconnect from this power. Therefore, there is always an underlying sense that we are more.

To not know what we are is quite mind boggling when you drill down to our true essence. How can something that is so amazingly complex and intelligent not know what it is? We, the Source of everything have chosen to experience not knowing ourselves. I don't refer to the 'ourselves' as the human aspect but as the power of all things that animates the human form. Why would it choose this? The Source wants to know this probability in endless probabilities. It chose a dense existence that represents separation in every aspect, beginning with the physical. It chose to gain knowledge of density in order to know Oneness through rediscovery – knowing darkness to understand light. Isn't this exciting? We have the opportunity to know unconsciousness and to discover our conscious selves. A game of hide and seek.

WE ARE 'ALL THINGS' - WE ARE THE SOURCE OF ALL THINGS

Remember that any separation that you believe in has been a story told to you by humans. Even the bible states that "ye are all gods" and "these things you shall do and more." And more? What part of that do we not understand? Who would teach anything that contradicts those powerful statements, instill fear and diminish the recognition of our power? Humans directed by the ego that benefit from controlling others with their usual tactics that have worked for centuries.

Why have we agreed to limitations? Fear. It is the emotion that humans have mastered. It is unlike anything we can ever experience as light beings and find ourselves fascinated with and somewhat addicted to it. It seems to hold great power when used on others because those others do not know that they are powerful beings and that nothing can truly harm them. It is fun for egos to play 'God' in the manner that is separate and controlling. Some refer to this energy field as 'evil,' but that too is more exploration of the One. The Source 'controls' nothing because it is that which explores, experiences and expands. It simply is. There is no judgement in this expansion. We are collectors of the experiences within probabilities.

As much as humans try to understand quantum physics, it is a futile quest as long as we approach it from our human mind. Not even Einstein embraced the interaction and effects humans had on energy. He referred to it as 'spooky action at a distance.' If someone that brilliant was not ready to accept our Oneness and mysterious powers, then certainly the rest of us won't find it easy. Yet he did acknowledge this 'spooky action' and if all things are energy and nothing is separate, isn't it a no-brainer that we would affect everything at all times?

Albert Einstein himself stated "I'm not an atheist, and I don't think I can call myself a pantheist... I believe in Spinoza's God who reveals himself in the orderly harmony of what exists, not in a God who concerns himself with fates and actions of human beings".

Your perceived individualism is an experience not to struggle with but to be celebrated and explored in all of its self-imposed limitations. Exploring limitations is also expansion because it contributes to the knowledge base of Source.

I know some extremely smart people who don't believe that human thoughts influence manifestations despite scientific findings. They view such connections as 'coincidences.' Even with all that we have discovered, no one has the answers to how the universe works simply because it is beyond human comprehension by design. We aren't supposed to know our Source in this role. It would take away from our search for solutions. As long as we masquerade as humans, we will not fully know those secrets. Fortunately, we don't need to know any secrets in order to access them. We do not have to 'know' anything because that knowledge exists within us. We must simply be at peace with 'being' that which is amazing, and the source of all things. All things are accessible whether consciously or unconsciously.

NOTHING, EVERYTHING AND ILLUSION

Let's be honest, this whole God thing messes us up. Is there a man in a robe off in a cloud overseeing us and deciding if we are worthy of receiving blessings? Is 'He' an angry God? Where did he come from? Why is He a HE or in human form as we often perceive? Our God has been a God that humans have placed in a box with a personality, an individual mind and body with human emotions and judgements. I think we know by now that none of this makes sense in a vast unlimited universe.

Is it possible that every 'thing' is not material at all? Can you release your attachment to the illusion and contemplate that the no 'thing' we believe is empty space is the 'all intelligence' that creates it?' This intelligence is the ultimate shape shifter that transforms into solids and non-material expressions. This is God.

Nothing is static. The seed evolves into the flower, blooms and returns back to the soil. There is no beginning nor ending to form which is a series of endless transformations in infinity. Nothing is one individual form except in illusion. The One is Source in eternal expansion. The God that we see as an individual is a story we created. As everything, Source cannot be a separate entity overseeing us. It is that and everything else.

If one believes that God is the energy Source of all creations and the creations themselves, then you and I are God. I do not refer to a person or single entity, but the energy Source of all. To claim to BE God is uncomfortable. When we hear such a statement, we usually cower in fear waiting for that angry lightning bolt to strike us dead. This is because in human terms, such a claim is perceived as one believing that they are greater than others and not the equal power that is all things. The human definition of God places us as disempowered lowly amoebas and God as some 'thing' out there that judges, punishes or rewards us. That is because humans think of themselves as separate from everything, especially one another. We can't even love our neighbor because of our differences much less think of them as part of the divine creation. As separate thinking entities, if you were to claim to BE God, the message is that you are claiming to be the ultimate separate power that rules over all things and that YOU are God and I am not. That is the human definition. That can never be true.

To claim to be THE God, THE power that resides over all others, is simply the ego manipulating other dense humans who keep looking outside of themselves for direction. We see such claims from cult leaders who place their powers and knowledge above others. When you realize that no ONE person or thing can be THE God because everyone is the ONE, you will find the glory in every creation. If you struggle with the 'I am God' statement, simply know that you are 'of God' that is everything we see and do not see. God is all things at all times, eternal, expanding, transitioning its' creativity into new energy forms. No one thing stands alone. We are Source. We are not equipped to understand it.

No one thing can exist independently making every creation of utmost importance. YOU are that important. YOU affect everything. Yes, EVERYTHING. There is no such thing as space and time. That 'space' you see is all intelligent, reacting to your every thought and feeling not as a messenger but as the writer, producer, and actor - you. It is you. Nothing on the other side of the universe is too far to be affected by your negative thoughts or your positive ones. Time and space are One. There is no distance that thoughts must travel because all 'happens' as One. Information is not transferred except within the illusion of thought. Our density allows a delay in our destructive choices so that we can play out the teachings they provide. If the matrix did not accommodate a delay in the transference of manifestation, every person who wished someone were dead would soon regret such a thought. The rules of our hologram allow for many other manifestation variables to come to the rescue of such directives. Otherwise, we would have destroyed ourselves long ago. This is the density that includes time and delays.

Within each creation exists entire universes. In essence, we are part of the body of One. Like a body that can transition but whose energy field never dies, the entire universe operates in the same manner. This is why we should never be concerned with the 'ending' of anything. In fact, we should celebrate the magnificence of the transition of all forms. They return to the original form of bliss before regrouping and launching back out into expansion.

When one knows his or her source, the façade of limitations becomes unrelatable. You are not one thing within creation. You are the One thing that is creation. Is the flower the petal, or the stem, or the dirt that it springs from? Is it only a flower if it consists of all of these things? Is it not also the sun that shines that keeps it alive, the rain, or the bee that pollinates it? After all, it is not a flower without these assets which allow it to be. Where does the flower begin and end? When it is a seed, is it still a flower or is it simply a seed? What is the seed? Is it the potential of the flower or a guarantee? When does the seed stop being a seed and officially the flower and what intelligence motivated the flower to become what it is in the first place? The ultimate question is 'why' does it bother to 'be' at all? The answer to that is an unending collection of knowledge through expansion.

You will find that there is no defined beginning nor end nor boundaries to anything. Everything relies on something else for its existence and evolved from something else. It then continues to evolve and transform into yet a new definition of itself, but still exists. Take 'you' for example. Are you this person you see in the mirror? If so, who was that toddler that you were at one moment in time and what were you before that? Were you the egg or the sperm? Are you both and if so, then who or what is YOU and what was 'that' before it converged to create you? What essence was it entangled with before it was that pairing contributed by your parents? There is no real YOU that you see in the mirror. Everything came from something else and that 'something else' is comprised of multiple other intelligent components seemingly separate yet all interconnected.

You are the nothing that is all intelligence and the something that it creates. That something that it creates is illusion which is also the One Consciousness because without the intelligence of the One, the illusion cannot exist. Something must then animate the illusion. Everything projected and manifested from the unseen One Consciousness is illusion. Why? That which it creates transforms and is never one permanent 'thing.' Illusions are the product of the One Consciousness playing with its unlimited power. This includes people, things, events, situations and conditions; everything. All are projections of a thought that originate from the One Mind. Each creation is not separate but is also the One, and remains an illusion until which time it intelligently moves on to another creation, another adventure. It then becomes a new illusion. Even higher beings in other realms are illusion. They too are an expression of Source.

If the One Consciousness IS and is perfection, why does it create illusions? While no human can ultimately answer this question, I will offer my truth. It explores all that it can be to know itself. It cannot truly know its light without knowing darkness. Only through this contrast of creations can it know its beauty. While it seems ridiculous to say that the One power that is everything seeks to know itself, the fact that it IS perfection is the reason it explores everything else. That exploration too, is all that it is in all expressions. It is not loss, but explores loss to understand wholeness. It is not anger, but explores anger to truly know love. You might say that it is curious, expansive, always in motion.

From our human aspect, the exploration of the pain we have endured makes no sense. Surely no good comes from knowing struggle. I assure you that what we have experienced allows us to know the glory of enlightenment in a way that we, as source, cannot know as total Oneness in its highest form. To just BE singularity is like being on a beautiful island with all of your needs being met, by yourself forever. How boring and how one dimensional that would be. Thrill and excitement come from the diversity of our experiences. When humans overcome struggles, the results are much sweeter. One cannot know wealth quite the same way until one knows poverty. Health is not truly appreciated until one knows illness. In fact, without our opposite experiences, we would not know these things along with the emotions that they inspire. These contrasts create a 'knowing' that is not possible without the extremes that illusion presents.

You are probably wondering how this helps you, the person who may be struggling with finances, relationships, depression or an abusive past. Even if you are on board with being this magnificent power of all creation, we are still dealing with playing out our challenging roles here. As I share with my students, disassociating with the persona you are playing allows you to become the observer. Instead of being that person that was abused, you can choose to see it as a learning experience to master because YOU are not that. You are experiencing that.

ILLUSION AND SOURCE SIMULTANEOUSLY

Now here is the tricky part about all of this Oneness that goes against everything most of us were taught. WE are that! Yes, YOU are THAT. God? Let us not use that all perfect and powerful name. Let us refer to the One of which all is created and exists as 'Source.' You don't just hold the power of Source, but you ARE that power and you are an expression of the power that is everything; one energy undivided. And if everything is God or Source, the One, or whatever name you choose, then YOU must be of the One, of God and not separate. You are the Source and the creation, the thought and the illusion. You are a seemingly individual expression connected to every other seemingly individual expression and beyond. It is impossible for you to be separate. You would not exist if you were because everything relies on something else, and something else, and then something else. It is infinite. But the most incredible part is that you are all of this simultaneously.

You exist in and are the same intelligent space as the matrix, the planet, other beings, Source. You are the power that is that space and the power that creates what exists within it. This power is ALL space, ALL events, ALL time and ALL probabilities at once. It is Illusion and Singularity simultaneously. It is ALL. You are that.

Our separate cloaks are unique and no two are alike. Isn't this fabulously creative? Feeling separate is such a foreign experience which explains why so many of us just don't feel very comfortable here! Have you ever thought "I just want to go home!" without knowing where 'home' is? This isn't home, yet at the same time it must be because nothing is separate. You occupy all space and time. So, wherever you are, is home but not your ideal one. Let's face it, we don't always like every 'home' we live in. So just have fun with it. It is a flash in eternity so don't waste it.

We are endless experiences existing as one, all affected by one another, all connected and responsible for its' whole and its' individualism. You see, you the person MUST be the power of the One because energy cannot be created nor destroyed. It always was, always will be. You always were, always will be and if you are not separate from the divine, you MUST be the divine.

YOU ARE AN ILLUSION IN THE ILLUSION THAT IS THE MATRIX THAT IS A DROP IN A SEA OF UNENDING ILLUSIONS

In order to be a player in the Matrix, you agreed to take on a role of illusion which is the persona you identify with today. It is your avatar. All players are illusion. Behind it you possess full power to manifest anything within the matrix rules. You are a creator of illusions within the matrix illusion. This is one of endless illusions we play out on other planets and in other forms and in other matrix illusions. All that you see that interacts with you is illusion from people to animals and plants and the planet you inhabit. Time is an illusion because everything is unending. What we perceive is time is like everything we abide by within the matrix. It gives us structures to work within. It allows us to know past actions that result in future results. At the core of everything is actually one power transforming in every moment, connected to itself in the forms of illusion that is the chain that is simply 'One Thing Happening.'

If we are in a matrix then what are the elements that are observable and interact with us such as other planets, stars and galaxies? Are they part of the matrix? After all, they affect our energy by way of their positions and orbits. Therefore, they must be a part of our matrix. If the moon can affect our oceans, then it too is part of our matrix. In fact, we would not survive without it. So, the question is, "how far does our matrix extend?" Everything participates in their own matrix that is illusion that overlaps with ours and everything else 'out there.' There are no defined lines between anything. Your energy field does not end with your body nor does it have a limit to how far it extends. You are meant to see yourself as a defined person. This is why our journey is so amazing. We live out our planned teachings believing that we stand alone. We are unaware that material creations are powered by the One energy field. Think of boats floating in an ocean. The ocean cannot be separated. It is one body of which boats float on. We are the ocean and we are the boats. Even those Extra Terrestrials that pop in and observe us are part of the One energy that is the ocean of which we float upon. They operate within their own matrix with rules, aware that they cannot interfere with our game decisions (except in exceptions that would affect the multiverse). Like your body, nerves do not stand alone, nor white blood cells, nor your organs. They are all connected and are a part of a bigger 'body' that has its own agenda. Nothing stands alone.

Now let us address that power that we wield. After all, if all is illusion and we are equal creators, one power, then we should be able to walk through walls. The answer is 'yes you can.' You have the ability to use it in any way you choose. The biggest challenge is to understand that you are always using it. Your thought, right now, is manifesting. Every thought is manifesting. By accepting to go into ignorance upon arrival to earth, we have no knowledge nor belief of this power that is always in action. The negative news, violent television show you watch, or virtual game where you kill others (a perceived enemy) is manifesting. By simply placing your attention on it, you bring it into your energy field wherein you become entangled and effects are in action.

The illusion of you gets to choose every step within its illusionary journey. Your beliefs in the illusion and how you function within it can reinforce pain or positive expansion. Choice is everything within the illusion. Our inability to walk through a wall is our limiting belief that human flesh and plaster don't mix. That would be true because both are operating on a dense level. We have the ability to transform into a more expansive and magical form of ourselves that changes the density of our energy field. This takes great knowledge and practice in human form, but can be done. It, however, does not serve the purpose of the matrix and is simply a fun distraction.

You may think, "if I can pinch my skin and it hurts, how can I be an illusion?" We relate illusion to virtual reality games to our current technology wherein no matter how 'real' it seems, there are physical experience limitations. I can 'see' things within my 5D technology but as of this writing, I will not totally physically feel that which I experience within my equipment. This is as far as the 3D world can take such experiences. However, in the unlimited matrix, we can experience so much more. Physical pain is part of this. While you can pinch your skin and hurt you are not that body. That is the illusion that you get to experience. And yes, it can hurt, sometimes unbearably.

Energy cannot be created nor destroyed. Therefore, if the 'you' that you relate to in that mirror has an expiration date, then what is that part that cannot be destroyed? The 'you' that cannot be destroyed is the energy, the light, that animates that body including the brain which is not the decisionmaker but the physical central command taking orders from the Mind of One. That persona you believe is you, is simply a costume of the role player that 'you' call Bob or Jane or Doug or Sandra. The energy that animates that body will always exist in some form. That is the form that walks through walls. The illusion continues in endless forms, and includes the physical pain that makes us believe that we are expendable. The 'you' you see in the mirror is the illusion and unlike what we name 'illusion' in our material world such as virtual games, the illusion of the metaverse has unlimited experiences. The light that experiences that is what 'is' eternal. The skin you pinch is part of the manifestation that is very real in the matrix you experience. YOU that is eternal is the light that animates all things. It is also the body, capable of density and physical pain.

When you see another 'illusion' you should remember that all of us will at some point transition into our original energy form. How will that illusion of a nasty boss or neighbor look then? Simply as light and perfection. All of the anger or frustration you had toward them won't make much sense as a light form. In fact, it will seem quite trivial except for the teaching that it presented. How are you handling your teachings and most of all, your teachers? Your greatest teachers are those who provoke you and not just those who share wisdom. This is the true test in our illusion of a 'self'. It is our attachment to this material body that fools us, makes us believe that we are all important and all that there is. Yet all of us know that our role will end at some point. Death of this illusion is assured for all of its players. Only your response to all of your experiences is what is crucial. No situation, event or pain is the problem nor the cause of your struggles. Your struggles are simply the resistance to it all. Your only assignment is to focus on your response to everything and everyone.

While quantum physics has verified that 'thoughts are things' and our very focus on any 'thing' has a direct effect on it, it doesn't begin to explain the source of all things. Humans simply aren't equipped to handle or process such information. This is by design in order for us to focus on our adventure here. To truly KNOW the source of all things is impossible because the mind in human form

47

that seeks to know is a limited mind. That in itself is a barrier to this information. And frankly, it would ruin the whole 'game' of being limited humans. Not so ironic and by design, our limiting thoughts are what allow us to experience the contrast of being human and this insane adventure we all chose. To know HOW this power works is baffling simply because we relate life to the material world that we see, and it is just so darned hard to get past that.

THE OTHER IS YOU

Humans are illusion. Think about it. If energy cannot be created nor destroyed, then it must transform. Therefore, you existed as 'something' prior to being a human. That 'something' is energy and that energy transformed into the physical form of you. So, what happens when the physical 'you' expires? You then become that pure energy once again. Basically, you are YOU again without the cloak. Even if you do not believe in reincarnation, can you explain how energy that always is, connects to you? It must be a form of that energy that creates various other forms that is illusion.

If you can be Bob, then Carol, a cat, an extra-terrestrial life form, a cloud or any number of expressions and everything is connected, then YOU must also be an unending timeline and the intelligence that creates it. In essence, you are the creative energy and the illusion. So, if you are the intelligence that flows through all things with no separation, then you and I are One. I am, in effect, you. We are the intelligence that continually creates and explores every form. WE are the force itself and the illusion that appears to be separate. When you look at the 'other,' you are looking at you. No, not YOU the human, but YOU the Force of creation, the One Consciousness that makes it so. The OTHER is you!

Think about the magnitude of this. You are energy and if you are also that energy which creates, this means that you have endless probabilities at your fingertips. Even as a seemingly limited, dense human, you can go beyond the perceived confines of the race because that One Consciousness has unlimited access to everything to alter its illusionary experience. Our consciousness

49

appears to experience one illusion at a time to know the individual journey with its individual choices. However, we are all things experiencing all illusions in one time, including all that has transpired, is happening, will happen, and can happen. This is too vast for humans to comprehend which is why we are created within limitations that cut us off from this knowledge. You get to be 'you,' the person with individual needs and desires, separate from others and a life unto your own.

Despite our designed limitations, all humans are capable of accessing the information of universal Oneness and its powers. This is done by shifting your energy frequency into a dimension beyond the body and into the formless quantum field. You may have experienced this leap into unfamiliar turf through astral projection, a dream that is more real than reality, or unexplainable contact from unseen realms. It may have come as a random and surprising mystical event. Perhaps you found yourself in a state of being wherein you existed in both the material and quantum field. Have you ever looked at 'the other' person and had a moment of a deep knowing that it was YOU that you were looking at? I have experienced this vast state of looking at another and seeing myself and the other through our mutual eyes. Because everything is energy, you have the ability to transport to any space and time within and out of illusion. This is accessible to all and does not require an enlightened state, however a higher frequency will connect you to your more expansive abilities. On occasion, there are openings which we may pass through, connected to the realms that exist outside of the matrix. We think of these as portals. Perhaps you know what I speak of and have never shared your experience for fear of ridicule. Do you ever feel the energy that emanates from the material world? I have known the unspoken communication and felt the waves of energy from the trees, the sun, and animals. I have instantaneously transported out of my body and observed myself while having a conversation with light beings. The matrix has passages and time glitches that are not mistakes but portals to the no-time that exist beyond it. We get a glimpse when we somehow align with these openings.

There is no human logic than can explain the glitches of time or other odd occurrences. Items in the illusion can disappear and reappear. Have you had this happen without any explanation? The cell phone sitting on your desk is gone and appears in the middle of your living room floor. The keys you placed on the table are no longer there but show up in that same spot you just searched. You seek a logical explanation but cannot. I do not refer to the bracelet that slipped in the couch cushions that shows up a month later when you vacuum. I speak of the objects that pop in and out of reality. You are not losing your mind. A shift occurred wherein dimensions and realities over lap and your item then exists in another dimension. Did yours come back? Mine always do. They reappear in the most amazing ways that are unexplainable. I find it fascinating and still wonder what prompts such events.

Items can also pop in and out with conscious directives. This can happen through interaction with entities on the 'other side.' My communication with my grandmother has produced astounding results. Once, in the middle of the room, an envelope appeared. I picked it up and found that it was a Christmas card from her that was a year old. She had been dead for months. In the card was cash. I don't know where it came from. Apparently, she gave it to me, but I filed it away. How did it suddenly appear after I happened to reach out to her during challenging times? She responded again when I asked her for a sign. It was the middle of winter with heavy snow on the ground. The rose bush I planted in her honor produced a red rose the next day. A seemingly impossible event. Or is it? She has demonstrated her support and awareness many other times, sometimes appearing in dreams to share messages. The veil between our worlds is thin.

Despite our ability to transport to other dimensions, you are here to play out 'you'.

Although the matrix has limitations which we abide by, there ARE some escape clauses which we will discuss later. They are safeguards put in place that protect the metaverse from the individual illusion's destructive acts. Within our matrix, you are granted free will and there is no situation that you cannot change. You are not confined to it, but to transport beyond it requires some knowledge and practice. The glimpses of other dimensions that you get along the way are to be enjoyed as reminders of what lies beyond our world.

Oneness is the theme for all illusions. We constantly expand outward to gather experiences and then return to the original state of One without illusion. Despite your individual free will gift to transform your own life within each illusion, your entire experience relies on others, your interaction with them and most of all your responses. Even when you make positive choices, you may blame others for not responding according to your rules. That 'other' so often gets in the way of our spiritual progress. If only they would get with the program, then we could all achieve utopia. This is the ignorant ego that has kept us at odds with one another.

Now here is when it gets tricky. To fully understand our roles here and our goal to awaken is to allow the 'other' their journey even if it is a destructive one. I don't refer to standing and watching self-destruction. There is a fine line between acceptance and complacency. You see, that 'other' provides the lessons and challenges that you may say is wrong and want to change. They are our ultimate teachers. My students struggle with this. Wanting others to be happy or awakened seems 'right,' but it is still the ego wanting the other to be different according to their beliefs about the situation. The message they send with their wishes for the best is 'you aren't OK.' That is judgement and non-acceptance. Yes, you want good things for them but that isn't what our earth journey is about. It is to experience unconsciousness and all of those unpleasant things the ego despises. To support 'the other' is to be OK with them and yourself. Yes, BE there for them, but not because you want to change them according to YOUR desires. Support them on THEIR journey. You ultimately cannot infringe on free will because everyone in every situation controls their thoughts and actions. If you offer assistance, you allow them choice. Can you be OK with that final choice they make? That response that is so important is to offer unconditional love and compassion no matter what.

Remember that all parties are working within one field of intelligence as one force. What each of us does, affects the whole instantly. Physical world results may take time to appear, but manifestation is always now. What you project through beliefs, thoughts and actions instantaneously manifests in some form. This reverberates throughout the universe. Therefore, that 'other' you disapprove of or ostracize is you, who will feel the effects in some form.

THE MATRIX

The earth matrix is one of endless matrix in the metaverse. Ours is designed to create opportunities through challenges. That is its sole programmed purpose. It is somewhat like an amusement park and planet Earth is the ride we hopped on. The matrix program is intelligent and taking directives as a part of YOU. Like you, it is an energy field and you are a creator of it, a player and an ongoing programmer. It is not a separate software installed by some outside source that controls humans, nor is it a punishment that some refer to as the 'prison planet.' It is a living, intelligent, fully conscious 'state of being' with agreed upon laws of which 'limitations' is primary. It is the pretend world that has specific rules like any game. Without rules, there is no structure nor meaning or objective - no challenges, nor goal to reach. Therefore, it presents a defined grid within which we operate. It is the play we wrote, produced and then starred in. It is the 'real' version of artificial intelligence that develops based on our input and use of it. It learns and adjusts according to that input. We are fully in control. Once we agree to participate, our role is chosen and the knowledge of our true form is then removed in order for it to be authentic, and the play begins. We go into unconsciousness which allows us to experience the density of the game. No outside source placed us in it nor controls outcomes. The play is flexible. The villain can become the hero unless the agreed upon role and goal is not in alignment with that. Anything is possible, like a dinner play wherein each evening a different actor is the murderer and the dinner is an open menu from which you choose.

All are equal in the matrix because Source is One perfect energy and cannot be anything else except through illusion. The matrix is that illusion although like everything, illusion is still part of the Source. It is not disconnected. Nothing is. Here, we experience inequality, disadvantages, prejudice, judgement, and isolation. How will I react when I believe another is inferior to me? Herein lies the test. The matrix allows me to believe that I am an individual island to myself and connected only to those with whom I interact. It allows me to judge another because I am not aware of our connection or that perceived imperfection itself is purposeful. We label one another and have opinions of what that label represents. We then respond accordingly without really knowing much of anything about that person because we do not see ourselves in them.

Once the agreed upon scenarios and lessons are in place, each wave of players makes its entrance into the program at their perfect designed times. The intelligent matrix aligns with the frequency of each. New players enter as organized connected 'soul groups' which then interact on various levels during their journey. It may be through friendship, families, organizations. There are no rules about this. They simply appear when specific tasks are to be completed. When higher frequency beings arrive, the game goes up a notch to even out the playing field. More light then shines within the darkness of the program to create balanced opportunities.

Some soul groups arrive in order to teach, to present openings to expansion, and demonstrate peaceful choices. Others here to assist in accelerating our progress may even present challenges. Not all are light beings arriving to save humanity. Humanity does not need to be saved. Each of us is totally capable and in charge of that. Challenges can be more impactful because they prompt great change such as major global events. Depending on the human response, these challenges can take the species to a more advanced level if we choose to evolve.

Each 'soul group' has a specific mission from the most subtle to global. This would be in the case of 9/11 and our pandemic for example wherein souls volunteered to exit during that time. Others come simply to raise the collective frequency. Their presence is all that is needed. Despite their level of spiritual advancement upon entry, all players, no matter what their mission, must step into unconsciousness and limitations. This assures that no one has an advantage. We then attempt to pass our tests and achieve our goals. Once in place, we are like divers who jump into the deep, endless sea to explore the unknown whose tanks of oxygen eventually run out. At the end of the exploration, we rise back to the surface to breath unencumbered, and perhaps to do it all over again.

Upon entry to earth, we take on veils of density, but never lose our light. That is impossible because light is the Source of all things. We are always fully intact. We simply obscure it, along with our knowledge. This is an unpleasant task, but fully necessary to experience the heaviness, hopelessness and disempowerment of the human role. This density is represented in the form of ego which every player takes on, despite their status prior to coming here. From there, the challenges begin. No matter how awakened the player, as long as they are participating in the matrix as a human, they continue to function in density. Ego and fear are a part of the package. This is the agreement in order to participate. Awakening simply means that fear and ego no longer dominate. They are used in a manner that benefits the collective which we will cover later on.

Even awakened humans find the matrix challenging. This is especially true because they must bear witness to great unnecessary struggles and pain from a loving perspective. Many believe that humans in ignorance are in the matrix and awakened beings are not. While higher frequency beings have one foot (so to speak) in the more expansive field, as long as they are humans, they reside in the matrix. It is the chosen game that provides purpose and a structure for all, no matter what level of spiritual evolution one achieves. Until every soul reaches enlightenment, the game will continue because it is a massively effective teaching platform with huge advantages. Humans get to advance their learning in unending ways because of the program. It creates opportunities and expansion into knowledge at an accelerated level. If all were to achieve enlightenment and catapult the species into the new world, the matrix as we know it would transform to another form of itself just as you do. When you are done with this game, and master it, you move on to another game with other rules.

Each player who enters the matrix comes with a set of pre-determined challenges. These are individual and collective. This cannot be anything but both because all actions affect and 'are' the whole. Not all opportunities will come in the form of unpleasant challenges, but the more progressive opportunities will truly be those that test the ego most. Mastering these is the whole point of the program. We then work within the matrix program to become masters over Illusion. Without a student, there is no need for a teacher. Without the ill, there is no need for the caretaker. The challenges we label as 'bad' are our opportunities to become the changemaker, nurturer and loving arms to another. As we evolve through higher choices within the more difficult challenges, we raise the matrix frequency and the game evolves with us. Like Pacman that presents a more challenging program as we master it, so the Matrix presents a more advanced life experience that holds more opportunities, breakthroughs and many rewards. Advanced players no longer struggle with the challenges because they understand their value and the positive returns that can result from mastering them. They learn to embrace the teachings and no longer fear them. The more we progress in the midst of this difficult game, the more we progress to new realities which, upon our transition, are reflected on that 'other side.' There are endless levels in those realms. Our choices determine everything from our life experiences, how the lives of others are affected, and all players in the universal illusions. Those who do not master their goals will not suffer upon graduation, but simply have to repeat a grade. There is no shame or punishment in this. Only learning.

Humans often refer to earth as the prison planet and we are the prisoners in a matrix that has been imposed and controlled by some evil outside source. This is a radically dense belief because Source is a loving creator and does not punish. It explores and experiences, therefore all facets of itself are doing the same. Nothing is imposed on anything or anyone without agreements by all involved. Once you understand that ignorance and ego is built into the game, you can understand why we automatically blame 'something else' for our undesirable circumstances. The ego sees it that way because it never takes responsibility for anything unpleasant. It places value on its personal gain and sees challenges not as opportunities but punishment, or something or someone else that needs to be fixed to suit its rules. Evil and control itself are created illusions.

Once one breaks through fear, the matrix purpose becomes very clear. Challenges are not setbacks, but more advanced opportunities. Each lead us to wisdom and the peace that knows nothing but unconditional love and compassion. The new job that you prayed for turns out to be stressful and not what you had hoped for. This is not a mistake. This is a new opportunity to perfect your manifestation. How could you have known unless you experienced it? Each experience is a stepping stone to expansion. The love relationship you thought you could not live without turns out to be abusive and now it all looks very different. It is all a continual learning journey taking you to new adventures that thrill, amaze, and yes, sometimes cause great pain. Without the unsatisfactory job, the new amazing one would not be as glorious. Without the abusive relationship, the new love would not be as appreciated or understood. All roads lead to advancement, especially the 'mistakes.' Because of these mistakes and our mastery, we are able to share with others and extend the caring that is at the root of our existence.

The matrix is the program and we are the programmers. Any prison that we perceive, we created by belief that somehow it has been created outside of our control or agreement to participate. The matrix in itself is not evil nor bad. Your human experience is not random. You do not have bad or good luck. It is all intelligently orchestrated yet malleable through what we have been granted as 'free will.' The matrix is a holographic program that offers the experience of density and darkness just as much as it offers love and happiness in a material world. It is the ultimate test of contrast within an illusion of limitations. How amazing to BE the power of the metaverse yet not know this nor believe it even when we are shown proof of it. Not even Christ's words "ye are all gods" has made the impact that was intended. We are that dense. What a mind blowing, wonderful experience.

One of the most frequently asked questions from my students is, "why would I choose this?" The next most popular statement is "I would never choose this!" There is total disbelief that any of us would agree to such pain and participate in the cruelty that others impose. In essence, it is allowed because WE allow it. WE are responsible because we agreed to density for ourselves and to participate in it with others. It is through choice that we reject to offer compassion toward another. We complain about planetary pain yet continue to support the infrastructures that create it through what we purchase and eat. We vote for, and hand our decision-making powers over to dense egos, believing someone else will save us. Our ego believes in right and wrong and both sides point fingers at one another with no behavior changes to resolve the issues. We see the other's unpleasant actions as a personal threat and do not see nor try to understand the fear and pain that motivates them. This is because we are in 'service to self' mode. We believe these humans are not deserving of our love and compassion because if they didn't behave so badly, our world would not be in such a mess when in fact, it is our love and compassion that holds the power to heal such pain and effect massive change. It is not 'them,' it is 'us' that continues the insane cycle of damage. "THEY" are the problem, while all the while we are in judgement which is an even lower frequency choice. This is the separation that must be overcome if we want to see the changes we came here to affect. This is the choice we can make that changes the world.

There is no Pacman game if those little minions don't pop out and gobble us up once in a while. That 'choice' that we made to come here was from a ten-thousand-foot view. In other words, things can look non-threatening and simple from a place of all power and knowledge. These decisions are made before ego and fear are installed. How else can we know ignorance and fear except to experience it first hand? We were not in the state of fear but of euphoria at the moment we chose this matrix. How tough could it be, right? We arrive not understanding problems, never imagining harming another or being harmed. Even though we 'know' this pain through past lives and the collective, we cannot know it while in our form outside of density. It is a distant memory that is easily resolved through the mind of Source. This is the mind of the child that enters the world with wonderment, who sees fairies and believes in magic.

We are one family that agreed to come here on a common mission and like most families, we don't always get along. But family is forever, and we find ourselves entangled in those relationships no matter how much we try to detach from the worst of them. The good news is that WE can end the conflict within our immediate and our global family. This is the ultimate goal of the matrix game. We can come together to experience the best of that dynamic family relationship creation – belonging, comfort, unconditional love, home, acceptance. Isn't that what we all desire? Isn't the ultimate condition to live in a safe home where you are loved, no matter what the circumstances, and all of your needs are met? It is the lack of this fulfilment that causes distortions in the human journey. We reflect that which we have experienced. Love reflects love. Abuse reflects more abuse, self-loathing and hate, and anger. It goes on and on until we say, 'no more.' We must break the cycle. Offering compassion to those who hold pain and strike out at us transcends all. Another's pain allows you to offer love beyond judgement because everyone deserves love. There is great beauty in this.

There were rules placed on all of us prior to entering this Earth hologram that go beyond the eight billion souls participating in this game. Our rules were self-imposed and in agreement with our galactic family. Yes, it goes beyond just being a human incarnating on one planet. All is a hologram from our planet to our universe. Within each energy field which is the expression of Source, the matrix sets rules for the game each participant must abide by. There are many beings involved in your incarnation decisions. Your body, parents, the challenges you will take on, and a personal mission is all laid out for you prior to your entry into the matrix. You are a part of this planning. Remember that nothing stands alone, therefore, nothing is imposed on you outside of your agreed upon participation. No one nor thing takes precedence over your journey or decisions because you and 'it' are one in the same. What we do on this planet reverberates throughout the One.

We are neither human nor individuals. We are the illusion of that. Illusion does not lessen the pain of this adventure which is a lot to bear. The big question is 'why would we agree to participate in this seeming hell?' What is the purpose of it all? As I discussed earlier, it is simply to know itself through contrast. New games, new challenges bring great excitement and learning. Hell is not imposed. It is a choice. From hell, heaven is then a choice. Of most importance, the more challenging the game you choose, the more you progress if you master it. It's like taking advanced calculus instead of basic math! You can't get into medical school with just basic math. What you accomplish here is of vital importance. While humans spend their lives trying to 'fix' situations and avoid what the ego considers uncomfortable or undesirable, they bypass the actual purpose and importance of it all.

Earth is one of the most exciting and advanced teaching experiences. One can accelerate wisdom and spiritual evolution by taking on its darkest personas. There is nothing to 'fix' because all challenges are by design. When one understands the matrix, it becomes an exciting place that plays out all that you forecasted and now must execute. That 'other' person that annoys and mentally tortures you is also by design. All of it is. Can you see it this way? If so, you can triumph and move into a higher realm that offers great rewards for your accomplishments.

The matrix does not end here. It extends beyond the planet. Those in heavenly realms (higher frequencies in light body forms) are aware of and relish the opportunity to assist us. We refer to them as angels, guides and guardians. They are not direct players but are in place to assist on the sidelines. It gives 'them' purpose and excitement too! It is an extension of the matrix with their own assignment. They are able to participate in endless programs simultaneously as do we, however they have an awareness of it.

The programs of illusion go on and on, extending to other beings, planets, and that which is unseen. Like the universe that actually has no 'line' that is drawn between it and the next metaverse, there are realms beyond that are nothing like the galaxies, solar systems and its planet dwelling creatures we associate with. Humans are on the lower end of the frequency scale. Our self-limiting beliefs about what exists 'out there' and more important, 'within' is what keeps us in turmoil and conflict. Limitations are human matrix creations and make us unique. Most other beings do not create such constraints and not all are granted free will either, which we will explore. Both conflict and peace exist throughout the multi-verse in the endless matrix games. Because Earth is on the lower end of the vibration scale, it is considered one of the greatest illusionary challenges. This is why we have 'back up' as part of the game that we can call upon. Have you ever played a game wherein the player must find the key, the sword, the gold, the magic wand that are used at specific critical times during the game to get out of a tight spot? This is how our higher beings fit in. Like the key or the magic wand, they are not handed to us to save the day but are tools that only we must find the use for and choose to activate when needed. This allows us to stay within the rules of free will, to learn our important lessons on our own while still receiving assistance when we are ready, have earned it, or it abides by our chosen path.

Imagine that anything is possible. Can you? That is Source. It simply wants to 'know.' What is 'that' which it is? It is like watching a movie without a challenge or conflict nor triumphant ending. Why bother? Emotions are the key to the human experience. They create our highs and painfully our lows in dramatic ways. How amazing to know pain, loss, and suffering when one has been living the peaceful, non-eventful movie. It is exciting because after the storm, the sun will eventually come out. Contrast. That is what the matrix program offers. This is what you desired to know and contribute toward.

Let us discuss that whole 'agreement' to be human. This particular matrix is a heavily challenging one for some of the best gamers in the universe. We opted to take on some of the darkest teachings. Some took on more than others. The payoff when mastered is great but who would guess that it could be so difficult?

63

After all, we are limitless. How bad could it be? It is like wanting to complete a marathon when you have never been a runner. No one can imagine how difficult it is to train, the pain as the lungs expand and struggle to get more air, the sore feet, aching muscles and hips. What about those who trek up steep mountainsides in sub-zero temperatures? It seems insane yet we do it anyway despite the risk to our lives. Why is that? Ah yes, there is that emotional 'high' of the danger. When we lack contrast, we become bored. All of this is the exploration of the dark and light within a dense environment. Some might call it 'hell' and we certainly can create that, but we can also create 'heaven' on earth. This is the ultimate goal, the triumphant ending, until another adventure begins.

Why does the matrix require that we not know our essence and unlimited powers? You cannot experience the thrill of contrast unless you believe that you are the separate, limited human that you see in the mirror. We hold the power to explore our darkness and destruction, yet never lose our essence of light itself. This is why it is possible for anyone to return to perfection – the process we call enlightenment. We never lost it. I am sure it is safe to say that you have always known that we were something more. It is this 'something more' that makes being human quite uncomfortable. A majority of humans never feel that they are home. Is this you? This adds to our discomfort in density and desire to escape it. Like Dorothy in "The Wizard of Oz," we always held the power to go home. We simply would not have believed it until we discovered it for ourselves. There is good news. We are discovering our source. It is then that the matrix will look very different, when struggle ends and transforms. This is the New Earth we speak of.

There is an older movie called "The Game." It stars Michael Douglas and Sean Penn. Michael Douglas is a wealthy business man, divorced and bitter. For his birthday, his brother, played by Sean Penn, purchases a real life 'game' of experiences presented by a company that is meant to create excitement through challenges.

Instead, things go very 'wrong' and Michael finds that he is losing everything important to him. His finances are taken over, house destroyed, and even his life is threatened when his taxi driver careens off of a bridge and plunges into the water where he barely escapes. These destructive events continue on to the point where he no longer wants to live. He has lost everything that he valued which he realizes ultimately meant nothing. Those close to him are now of most importance and whom he must now rely on to survive. It is at this moment that he has an epiphany. We refer to that as 'the dark night of the soul' when one either departs the planet or becomes renewed. Contrast. Believing he has lost all, he jumps off of a building only to be saved. The game ends. He is captured in a safety net surrounded by friends and family who receive him with great love and celebration. It was all planned to take him to an awakening. He gets it. It was not until he physically experienced loss and believed it to be real that he transformed. You don't want to miss that do you? It cannot be duplicated in our light state. This is our matrix that takes us to the brink of darkness.

You may be wondering 'what if I don't triumph?' What if you don't forgive the unforgiveable, or overcome the depression, get over the pain of a cheating spouse or the resentment toward an abusive parent? The list goes on. Your story does not end with one game. The matrix program continues to run and like Pac Man, you regenerate and start the game over again. There is no ending nor judgement in regard to your progress. There is only transformation. You cannot make a mistake.

FREE WILL

We all know what free will means, although students sometimes confuse it with the physical force others often impose. Physical conditions that restrict us do not limit our free will. Most humans believe we are 'losing' our free will when this happens, but that can never be true. No matter what occurs in the matrix, you can always believe, think and act according to your choice within any situation. The physical world cannot stop the free will of the players. This is what make us so powerful and dangerous. We are allowed to destroy others and ourselves.

There are endless illusions and free will is incorporated into ours to offer the ability to oppose one another. Free will on a dense planet creates the greatest of challenges because it allows players to annihilate one another. Unconscious players are allowed to act individually and make decisions that have dire consequences. This is intentional because it creates the most dangerous causes and effects that can take us into that dark place we name 'evil.' Evil is not imposed, but a choice; a creation through free will.

Let us explore the term 'free will' and what exists outside of it. We cannot imagine an existence without free will. Not having free will surely must be a prison-imposed way of life, but it is actually the opposite! One might think that not having free will means that something or someone is dictating the actions and circumstances of the players. This is not the case, because beings that do not have free will function on a much higher frequency. Planets operating on matrix programs that do not have free will simply operate as One mind. There is no reason to install free will because the Whole of their collective is in alignment and does not oppose itself. They do not operate as individuals or possess egos that choose conflict. Separate choices are not necessary because nothing is to be learned from it within their game. They are on an advanced level past the teachings that free will offers. They act in unison and in peace, placing service to others first, which is the ultimate goal of the Earth Matrix. One mind does not require free will.

Free will offers the opportunity for humans to transition into the state of One Mind and 'service to others.' Our individual choices can take us back into unity, our ultimate goal. The endless explorations of hate, opposition, greed, power and all that uses free will to separate and destroy us are the challenge to be overcome. Free will, like fear, are attributes of the game that all humans can break through to the understanding that it isn't necessary. It is illusion. We lose nothing when we give up free will. We gain everything when we operate as a unified light. There, all needs are met.

HOW MANIFESTING WORKS

We really like the material world when we 'have it.' We 'desire' things. We see what is out there and trust the physical over the unseen possibilities. Where does that unseen exist anyway? We continually stop our desired manifestations in their tracks when they don't appear according to our material world rules because the moment that we doubt that we are creators, it grants our wish of limitation. Our power is beyond comprehension. Even enlightened humans do not have this information simply because to be enlightened means not requiring to 'know.' Those who seek it will never find such answers and those closest to them do not require them.

However, being in an awakened state allows amazing manifestations with a simple thought because it is a space of no barriers.

The most difficult truth for dense humans to comprehend is that they are creating everything even with unconscious thoughts. The mind is the tool that allows us to do that. I do not refer to the brain, but the central creative energy that connects the physical with the quantum field. The illusion of separate humans is created in order for us to have perceived individual experiences. Your mind directed to your experience will create a different reality to mine. No two realities are the same yet interact with one another. Our powerful gift as humans resides in our ability to create. This power is to be discovered and one of the critical objectives of the game because once claimed, everything changes. No lack, sorrow, anger, illness can exist at that point and heaven on Earth is achieved. Game over.

The good news is that it is not necessary to know WHAT or HOW the universe works in order to access the amazing powers of creation; your powers. This power is in constant motion with or without our conscious direction. When humans release the desire to know and control, they embody the One in its highest form. To release the desire to understand that which is not understandable is called faith. Faith is knowing that we ARE. I AM. I am that, I am. No further explanation is required. From there, all things are possible. So, you see, you don't need to KNOW anything. You just ARE. There is no secret or formula nor technique. Everything that you 'truly' need whether in the form of a lesson, a situation, gift, a relationship all flows to you in divine time because the 'all intelligent' quantum field always gives you what will expand your knowledge and take you to higher choices. It is what you desire even if you don't recognize it now.

Manifesting is such a huge, popular subject because it is inspired by the ego that 'wants' something. That 'something' will surely fix our problems. However, in my years of teaching, I have seen a consistent pattern with the use of manifestation techniques that demonstrates that 'how' we manifest and where we come from within the field to manifest, directly affects the outcome. Although I teach manifesting on an advanced level, there is a very important component to achieving successful results. One must come from a creative and giving space of non-attachment and not a material one. In other words, we can easily manifest even impossible things, but if we are not coming from a higher frequency, it will not satisfy. I will give you an astounding example of this.

One of my new students explained his very unhappy situation that he wanted me to fix with my manifesting knowledge and techniques. He wanted to know how to manifest money to fix his life along with eliminating people who were causing great irritation. The astounding part is that years ago, he studied law of attraction 'techniques' that resulted in a $10,000 lottery win, and TWO $1 MILLION dollar wins within a three-year period. Pretty astounding indeed. You might ask what on earth could he want after such a windfall? Plenty.

You see, although the money certainly satisfied a short-term desire, it was soon gone as it is with most lottery winners, and he was back in the world of challenges. A series of events then brought him physical pain and disabilities. A love relationship tortured him for a decade. A neighbor whom he got evicted for being disruptive purposely tortures him daily with loud music. His solution was to manifest that these things change in his favor. It was then that we had a serious talk. What he did not recognize was that he was getting exactly what he needed to go into that happiness he was seeking.

The 'field' was giving him messages that he had not recognized. "Stuff never satisfies." This three-time lottery winner was now even more unhappy than ever. Oh sure, I know what you may be thinking – "That wouldn't be me!" Depending on your starting point, it most certainly could be you. You see, the material world does not change your frequency status. His money paid off a mortgage, but it didn't 'fix' the world that he chose to create and participate in. He still had to deal with his view and approach of the world and that is what dictated the manifestations he lived in. It was now time to work on that.

Here is where it gets tricky. When one is in a heavy ego state, it has no desire to work on releasing that ego that wants even more control when it's unhappy. It continues to want the quick fix even when every result has proven that it never lasts. It is satisfied with short-term highs, hoping that the next one will stick. His desire was to eliminate the 'problems' instead of facing why they appeared in the first place. Every unhappy situation was due to the world 'out there' and 'they' should change according to his ego's rules. The neighbor was the problem for him because he did not choose compassion to understand the source of his behavior. He did not see the fear and anger this person was facing now that he was evicted. Even though the situation was a self-inflicted result, the student disregarded the source of the behavior and was focused on service to self. The millions did not fix his unhappiness, but he was not exploring the peace that he could experience with or without it. He was deeply entrenched in the dense, material world concerned only with what 'I want' and what 'I get.'

This student was not a 'bad' person according to human labels. He was giving to others including homeless or those in need. On further examination, his giving came with rules. When one did not behave in a manor he desired, he referred to his 'giving' as backfiring. The ego always has rules to giving. It always wants something in return on its terms. Yes, even when it gives. The most challenging part for me as a teacher is to help students to recognize that their entire reality is being controlled by the ego's rules. They want me to 'fix' their unhappiness with more techniques. I am sure that there is great disappointment when I assign practices that do not include conjuring 'things' or 'people' to come to their rescue. That is reserved for advanced students who apply their manifesting skills from a high frequency. It is from there that they are most powerful.

The student worked on going into compassion and meditated with my "One Consciousness" meditation and within three days of our session, the neighbor left his residence. Astounding? Not really. The focus on conflict and the 'problem' had ended, and so did the source of it. The source was the student's struggle and conflict. This is how simple it is. The same happened with another student who had great conflict with a co-worked. After our session, she went into work with a compassionate and clear energy field. She shared that it was an amazing day with no conflict and that they actually worked, for the first time, as a team. When our problem stops being a problem, it stops being a problem. The circumstances will then dissolve and give way to something new and more expansive.

We 'desire' things and believe the present situation of the material world and not the unseen probabilities. If the situation is dire, we are even less likely to envision a positive solution because we are reacting to the painful one at hand. It is at this point we are in a low frequency, and less likely to change the situation. This is because a specific belief has taken us there in the first place and to change it would require an understanding of its appearance and a mind shift to change it. This is at the core of our limitations. What we believe we receive and our thoughts about that tend to remain the same. In addition, we rarely believe that we created the perceived problem.

I have taught students how to "Break Through Fear" for years with 5-star ratings. They have experienced clarity, happiness, new jobs, higher paying careers, happier relationships, new homes and better health. This has been consistent and has not taken long periods to achieve. Why aren't more people flocking to learn how to break through the limitations that are self-imposed in order to live amazing lives? What is it about humans that keeps them choosing suffering over joy, health, and abundance? Belief. Funny how we keep coming back to that, don't we? Those who do not pursue my teachings often do not believe in their ability to turn any life situation around. It is as though we are addicted to suffering. We fear giving up fear. It is what we know, and humans love familiarity. Just introduce change to a human and watch the resistance.

Change is required to achieve one's goals, yet change is the enemy even when positive outcomes are available. Let's refer back to lottery winners. A vast majority lose their fortunes. They simply have not learned how to be wealthy. They cling to the old ways, believe in limitations and lack, and thus recreate them. This is why manifesting that which is different to our current circumstances is so difficult. We unknowingly self-sabotage our dreams and return to old beliefs and patterns that then manifest. "See? I knew it was this way!" we state, when things go right back to lack, or struggle, or the relationship fails. We had simply slipped back into old thinking which created as ordered. So often the manifestation was created from 'need' or desperation, or believing that it would solve a problem or supply happiness. The resulting manifestation is materially temporary, and the core of its energy field becomes apparent. A lower frequency manifestation will not bring lasting happiness nor abundance.

Manifesting is not something we do when we 'want' things. It is what we do 24/7. WHAT we manifest is a result of a belief that results in a thought that results in an action, and manifests. This goes on in every moment whether we are awake or asleep. Everything appears in the material world from this formula and until the directive is changed, will remain so. This is why we find it difficult to change circumstances that we have endured our entire lives. Despite our desires to change them, the patterns of beliefs, thoughts and actions are the same and thus the results are the same. Any wishes for something different have no power over our 'request to the universe' in the form of our beliefs that override all else.

Go ahead and make those vision boards, light candles and insight incantations. None of it will change your reality until you change the beliefs underlying your desires. In fact, if looking at a picture of a desire invokes disbelief, you are actually creating more barriers to receiving it. "There it is! I want it but I'll never have it!" – is the message. This is why so many become frustrated at their attempts to manifest specific goals. They are not paying attention to their feelings and believe that an outside power will somehow grant their wishes, overriding their own disbelief. Will it show up? Only if the mind truly knows that the probability exists and that he/she has chosen it. Waiting for something else to make it happen is a message of "I am not in control" and so it is. And as stated earlier, if we believe that we can have a specific thing or situation, we aren't changing our realities to accommodate it. So, the old thoughts of lack or low self-esteem cancel it out and bring back what we truly believe.

Exactly how does one change all of this? After all, conditioned thinking rarely changes in an instant and we simply do not believe we are the creators of the circumstances in the first place. And if thoughts are things, we have an even bigger problem because we don't recognize that we are having negative thoughts most of our day. Letting go of control is the last thing that the ego wants because if things are not to our satisfaction, it believes that letting go would surely produce worse results and so the cycle continues.

Your first step toward real control over your manifestations is through letting go of all that you believe is true and questioning everything that you thought was how the world works. The universe is more expansive than our brains and will always have bigger plans for us. It holds all probabilities. Through the universal mind we can access this information when the limiting and controlling ego steps aside. We ARE that which we desire and our 'higher self' will take charge if we allow it. It is this 'letting go' that allows that higher self to then put everything into action. Humans cannot know what that entails and so stepping back and simply 'knowing' it is done without judgement or analysis puts higher manifestations into action. I assure you that when you truly go into that space of 'allowing,' manifestations will appear that will amaze you. In fact, you will receive many gifts that you didn't even realize you requested in the power of this 'letting go.'

Humans operate in the reverse order of how 'things are.'

We are not the material world. We are creators of the material world.

We have no limits and create with a thought. All thoughts create. There is no effort in this, only focus.

We never need struggle for 'anything.' Everything exists and we merely choose.

We are THAT which is 'out there.' We are everything and create everything. Choice pulls it into our experience.

We do not have to 'ask' an independent power. We are the energy of all that we desire.

The biggest challenge for humans is to end beliefs of separation of anything – others, their power, and the quantum field. Through separation, we cannot consciously access our power because we continually think of it as something that has independent thoughts and decision-making. It is a virtual waiting game that sometimes produces the desired effects, but in most cases does not. When we look outside of ourselves for answers, our statement is 'something else will grant this' and therefore, that is exactly what we create. We then wait, and wait.

THE SPACE WHERE MIRACLES RESIDE

There is a space where miracles reside. It is the high frequency where ego cannot live. The opening is through a release of thoughts and expectations which are replaced with hope and faith. It is the realm where all beings have no label, are one, equal and perfect. There is nothing to heal. Miracles are simply a return to original form whether physical or situational. The veil of imbalance is removed, no longer needed, no longer held by a belief. This is not a decision made by a separate power, but the acceptance of that perfection by the recipient who IS the shared creator.

This takes us back to the suffering that created the physical or situational challenge in the first place. Did we create it for a purpose or was it an unnecessary fabrication? Most likely both because nothing goes without intelligent purpose. Even 'mistakes' are our learning and the gathering of experiences. When we are ready to release these lessons, we can move into the miracle space where the perfect person appears in your life, the ideal job, the money arrives, and the spontaneous healing occurs. I have experienced these miracles and you most likely have too. Everyone has access. It is another choice, not to avoid the challenges or lessons, but to release those lessons when no longer needed.

Challenges are literal and you may not know their origins. Because you are eternal, your history is also eternal. It all exists in the now. The choices of millions of non-existent past years are with you now. If you have not mastered abundance, or compassion, or self-love, then you may be challenged in this life with these situations in order to finally conquer them. If you have back pain, the foundation of your life may not be in order. If your knees or feet hurt, you may be heading in the wrong direction in life. If you contract cancer, you may have anger and have internalized feelings that have caused your body to stop working in harmony. While these examples are not always true, we often find that there is a direct correlation with our life problems and the symptoms that reflect them. I have found that symptoms correlate with my students' issues and that they can be eliminated.

Everything can be changed in an instant. There is no ongoing punishment for past decisions as we are told. Those on the cross next to Christ were forgiven simply by asking. The same applies to you. But remember that asking does not make it so. You must believe and truly release everything you thought about yourself and others. Know that you must simply hand over your pain and receive the return to your perfection. This is when a miracle appears. Perfection is recognized and negative beliefs are dissolved.

YOU CAN CHANGE YOUR PAST

Regrets are negative energies that we create based on our thoughts about our choices in a 'time' that we feel can never be changed. In fact, your choices today can actually change the past. All 'things' exist simultaneously. Illusions are endless personas playing out endless probabilities that are not 'created' but exist at all times. Our focus through beliefs, thoughts, and actions bring each probability into our own energy field of events. You alone do this.

Time stumps our logic and challenges our imagination. There is indisputable proof that the future affects the past equally as the past dictates the future. This has been demonstrated for decades but is not an easy concept for linear thinking humans. It IS possible that a future YOU that does not look like you at all, can visit the YOU that you are NOW. It is possible that everything you do NOW can change the past. This is why so many predictions by very talented and viable prophets have not come to pass. Reality is malleable because reality as we perceive it simply does not exist in the static, unchangeable way that we imagine. There is no one destiny. There is no outside force that determines your future. There is only YOU. There is only ONE and that ONE is the past, the future, the present, everything that ever was and ever will be, it is the material and non-material creations, and is the power and the intelligence directing it all. You are that.

This is an important subject because no matter how much you understand your power, there is an energy frequency created by your past experiences and your reaction to them during that time period. That frequency rests on what you believe about it and from there we bring it into our present. This energy goes deep, and the only way one can change one's past is to change the story about it. This is the awakening that finds purpose in all and is thankful for the teachings of the past. The past that you may blame is what you chose to conquer by choosing different responses than the collective has chosen. It is never too late to change your past.

What are you carrying with you that is a result of past pain that you feel is the result of the actions of others? What is that story you tell yourself about it? Does it permeate your life and control your responses? Does it create limitations, self-sabotage, or fear? These are stories, not your past. If it was your past, then it would be impossible to change the story and see it differently. You can change the stories and turn around how you see everything. Thus, when you change the story, your past completely changes. You can see your past as a huge gift and a teaching you took on to master. Did you master it? Did you choose the example of Christ to take on something deeply painful and to love and forgive anyway? This is the ultimate awakening.

Would you like to change your past and to be free of dense frequencies as a result of it? Would you like to make sense of past pain and any stories you chose about it? They may be the ones you created about yourself, or what has been inflicted on you by others. This matters not. The story can change because only the ego feels damaged. When you release the ego's beliefs that it has been wronged or that it is not good enough for this world, or that what it has done is unforgiveable, all energy transforms. It literally shifts and from there, you the creator, decide what comes next. Will you master this teaching and love the other and yourself? Will you be grateful for the experiences that are so much bigger than you can imagine? Is there humor within the scenario when you examine your response that was 'so serious' and maybe even frivolous? Of

79

course, there is. Laughter is dominant in the quantum space where nothing is taken quite so seriously.

Let us address that bigger picture. Everything is expansion, contributing to the experience of the whole. How can there be good or bad if all things come from the loving creator? It cannot oppose itself. That opposition is an illusion of conflict which is another experience One chose to know. Every creation you see is a part of that expression carrying out its assignment. Everything you choose, feel, and believe is a part of the expansive One 'knowing' limitless creation with no ending. Yes, all that you choose is THAT and THAT can't be wrong, if only named by humans which is just another experience – right and wrong. You are that important. You are simply carrying out your agreed upon orders to contribute to expansion. From there you continue on to new experiences that are determined by your choices guided by the last one. This is why you should be inspired to change your past stories and the meaning you gave your human journey. Are you ready?

What would be the most expansive, meaningful lesson you could apply to any pain you experienced? What story can you change about your past including beliefs about yourself that are not kind? Compassion and love are available for everyone, no matter what you have done. Move past forgiveness and see that no one makes a mistake. They are players in expansion. Your tormentor is your teacher; the one who gave you 'choice.' Will it be love and compassion or will you continue to cling to the material world that generates pain on demand? It is loaded with that experience, but equally presents triumph over it.

Everything you believe is true – for you. Your pain is a result of your experience and struggle is a result of your story about that pain which you labeled 'wrong,' having no value or meaning. In order to change this, the story must change. Your entire perspective on life as a human, rests solely on what you accept as your truth. Can pain have value? Of course. We know that when one is physically ill, only then can he or she know the beauty of health. When we carry a story of being 'wronged', that pain lives with us and literally resides within our energy field and our physical body. Cancer is often linked to anger as are other illnesses. Negative thoughts create an imbalance and our bodies are then no longer working as a community and go into conflict, mimicking the individual's energy field.

Suffering is not necessary. Changing the story about your past does not excuse another's behavior. Cause and effect is very much in action with us all and they will reap the consequences of their cruelty. Will you also reap the consequences of your anger and blame or worse, judgement? Yes. This is why it is so important to allow others to make their choices, learn from them, and know that the greater power takes care of everything. Punishment comes in the form of having to know the pain we inflicted on others. Will you continue to carry that pain also? It serves no good purpose for you or anyone. The collective will, however, experience the release of that pain, your compassion, love, and forgiveness if you are not ready to accept that all is as it should be. In that case, forgiveness will do just fine.

CHOICE

Humans are not programmed to understand their Oneness. Isn't this fascinating? This is what makes YOU so unique. You chose the most challenging of experiences! Forgetting allows for the great follies that we create, the contrast that causes pain and then, hopefully, understanding and awakening. The ultimate 'letting go' of our stories and individual truths will take us closer to singularity. Until then, we are allowed to know good from evil, prince from pauper, pain from joy, and love. Forgetting allows us to know the euphoria of the higher self because until we have experienced everything that is NOT that, euphoria is not understandable. Without contrast, we cannot know our greatness. This is God. This is the One. Humans struggle with this explanation because we are told that we are not great, and this is why we are so fearful to claim it. We are told it is wrong and that we will be punished for such thoughts. Of course, this belief has been created by humans and part of those 'limitations' we have put in place. Therefore, it cannot be trusted. The bible, however, states that WE are all Gods and those miracles Christ performed? Well, wasn't it he who said, 'These things ye shall do and more?" Didn't he walk on water and heal the sick? Whom do you choose to believe?

Our biggest fear is that we are powerful beyond our comprehension and that all we have experienced and ever will has been created by us. This means that we are totally responsible for everything both good and bad and there is no other person or higher power to blame. Knowing our power means that all we have clung to in the material world is fluid and a result of this power that each of us alone has projected. Our lack, good fortune, illnesses, are all generated by us. Claiming our power means that we are the source of all that we blame for our circumstances and all that is rewarded. It is frightening because it means that we are alone in this power and great responsibility and nothing outside of us will 'save' us because WE are the 'something outside of us.' We are always choosing whether through beliefs, thoughts, or actions and especially through our responses to the choices of others. You always have choice.

The only barriers to manifesting desirable circumstances is disbelief of this power and our denial of the outcomes we create from our directives. When 'things go wrong,' we deny that we were the source of the results, not understanding what they can lead to. Manifesting is a constant activity. You are manifesting at every moment. When you sleep, you manifest. When you work-out, eat, and work, you manifest. Whether consciously or not, you are manifesting. Every thought and action contribute toward your world and all of your results. Even if believe in your ability to manifest certain outcomes, your feelings don't lie. The belief in the outcome itself, either way, is what manifests. No mantra will manifest your desire if you do not believe. This is choice and you can change it.

Humans walk around like unconscious robots that are programmed according to their outside world. They unwittingly create their world, complain about it, are focused on dissatisfaction of those results and through that focus continue to create more of it. No matter how often they are shown that the 'outside world' is being created by them, they refuse to believe it. It is too frightening to admit such power and easier to blame others. We are in a fog of density so thick that we can't see through it. We feel weak, vulnerable, impermanent and want 'someone' or 'something' to make it all better. There is no escaping our responsibility for what is. We might as well claim it and start using it in magical ways. If only we could see through the veil of the ego. It isn't easy to let go of an old friend even if that friend has not been kind. Familiarity is easier than change.

We can change any circumstance. Why, when we now know that 'thoughts are things' and our human façade is not who or what we are, do we continue on with those limiting thoughts and actions? Humans, the heavy ego vibration of this creation, are lazy. We are conditioned to believe that good things require great effort. We want 'someone' or 'something' else to handle everything for us, which is why when things go wrong, we shout out in prayer for a solution. We love the idea of 'ask and you shall receive.' It allows our lazy ego to place an order, sit on our butts and wait for the delivery. The truth is that we are asking THE power, which is ourselves and if we don't get off of those butts, gather the items, prepare and cook them, we aren't eating. Every step of the manifestation process is 'us.' This idea exhausts the ego which is the root of ultimate disempowerment. This too, however, is illusion but granted through belief.

Be it God or the quantum field, or whatever you believe, eliminating a separate thinking entity that grants your desires is a total turnaround in everything we have been told exists. Taking responsibility for our triumphs and our woes is a big deal. Humans love to celebrate triumphs by believing they somehow deserved it, and blame their woes on punishment bestowed upon them by that same judgmental ultimate force, or more often 'unfairness.' That huge, unlimited power is a lot for us to comprehend. It is overwhelming and facing that fact means that everything you have not been pleased with in your life was YOUR creation; YOUR choice.

The most exciting fact about our power is that everyone has it. Everyone has it because everything is simply one energy. There is no judgement or imbalance of this power. Only our use of it can cause an imbalance which is perceived, and part of that free will gift I covered earlier. All humans are equal in the universe. All power simply 'is.' The yin and yang are the duality that balances out the experience of illusion. There cannot be a savior without a fall.

Humanity has been programmed to believe in limitations through its own choice. Earthlings are a demonstration of imbalance of all things. Our perceived limitations form the basis of our history and how we operate. Humans who are aware of their true power have all too often used it to control others whom they convince are powerless and limited. If you believe you are limited, you create it. That is how powerful you are.

What if you had to take responsibility not only for your past, but your future? Is this difficult for you? If so, then you are still in disempowerment and thus that is your directive to the universe. Perhaps you are saying "I am not afraid to claim my power." Perhaps you truly do feel you have claimed it. So, I will ask you, "Are you using it in the manner you desire?" Are you in a peaceful place, manifesting from there? Or do you feel like things just 'happen' and you don't know why. Perhaps there are things and situations that you desire and have not quite achieved? It is possible that you don't truly claim your power in the manner that is possible. You may be thinking of yourself as a flesh and blood being that has great limitations and 'power' is supernatural and something that has to be learned.

Miracles would have no real meaning in a world that utilized its full powers. Miracles would simply be every day events. Healing, abundance, inventions, and inspiration would be just what we do. Using our true powers would take humanity to a state of "heaven on earth" if used for positive purposes. So far, it has had the reverse effect because we deny them and direct them in fear. Utilizing our full potential does not guarantee a world of peace. Only service to others will do that. Being human is that state of free will within all frequencies. You choose your frequency. No one else can do that. Heaven on earth would mean using our powers beyond the dictates of the ego and here is the test of the human experience. Not only are we challenged with remembering our powers, but also to use them to overcome the density of the species by placing 'being human' aside.

Christ told us that we too could perform miracles and more. Words from the most profound teacher who ever walked our planet did not penetrate our ignorance. Why don't we believe? What stops us from claiming our power? Fear. Our biggest fear is that it is wrong to claim such powers because we continue to believe in separation. We continue to separate ourselves from the very person who demonstrated and told us that we too hold this power. Does this sound insane? It is, but not when we understand the history behind this belief. The human conditioning is powerful because it uses that same power to create our own limitations. Those who understand our powers have used them to convince others that it is wrong to believe such things and teach separation. The ego believes that power is not equally distributed and that there are those who 'rank' higher amongst humans in those abilities.

Ego is destructive because it is threatened by 'others' and therefore will do everything to maintain its own control and keep them powerless, or at least convince them that they are. What a better way to do this than to use fear to convince the masses that it is wrong to think that they hold limitless powers. It is even more convincing when religion-based teachings tell us that we are condemned to think that we could possibly hold powers equal to that of Christ despite his own declaration that we do. Isn't denying His words blasphemous? Why do we continually believe the word of man over God. Man is the individual, the ego and the density. God is truth and love, power and miracles. We are of that and have never lost access. The connection is eternal with all creations.

86

This human experience is simply a play, an adventure exploring limitations. However, we are seeing more and more that we are capable of miracles and that there is a directive behind them which we control. Miracles are not random. They too are a choice.

The human condition is habitual choice of suffering through self-destructive beliefs and behavior despite what we discover about our powers within the quantum field. This conditioning has been our biggest barrier. However, there is wonderful news. A great awakening has been underway and reached a tipping point. What is that tipping point? Enough humans are realizing that we are much more, and that suffering can end. We see positive transformation taking place all around us and now we are seeing it within ourselves. We are choosing a new pathway, despite the condition of our physical surroundings and recognizing that we have created it all, and are individuals contributing to a collective. We are all responsible. We are stepping outside of the control of others now that we recognize that they too have been asleep in ignorance. We are ready for a new earth and ready to take on the role of change makers. We have come to our own realization that we are, we must be, much, much more than these bodies.

If you continue to experience fear of your future or lose faith that your life can change, you are among the majority that doesn't truly believe. Belief in our power is discouraged but I assure you that these powers are not reserved for the likes of Christ, Buddha and other super powers. While they certainly were special powerful beings, they did not hold any more gifts than you do. However, they did come to demonstrate that it can be done and that YOU too are a special powerful being. How can we be anything less when all is One? How can we question the words of the Ones who have demonstrated those powers and cling to the corrupt words of dense humans? Insanity indeed.

Humans. We are an enigma in the universe, designed to know the depths of the dark side so that we can know our light. It is the most difficult choice any energy field can make. When in our natural state of pure light, we cannot imagine the depths of the limitations that we feel when we are here. Only a human body can create this kind of pain. You truly are amazing to have come here. Thank you for being such a bold and courageous volunteer.

As I lounged on my deck today, I watched a young family on the property behind me playing. A little boy was running as each parent chased him. The father hid behind a tree and the little boy found him and laughed loudly. The mom then ran away from the little boy and he, understanding the game, chased her. She hid behind a tree of which he surely saw yet still ran after her as though it was all a surprise. He laughed loudly when he discovered her as he had throughout this entire game. There was no disappointment from the little boy by knowing exactly where his parents were hiding. He knew that the 'make believe' of it all was the best part and enjoyed the discovery just the same. None of it was truly a surprise, but that didn't change his reaction. He understood the joy in the game of which all players agreed to share. All playing 'roles' of make believe that produced positive results for all involved. This is exactly how life works. We can 'know' the 'pretend' of it all and find the joy in the game, or battle this experience that doesn't seem to make much sense most of the time.

All too often, we struggle with our roles, never satisfied with them and wanting to play 'another's' role. Surely that 'other' has it easier than you. We lose our sense of adventure and discovery when we battle with 'what is' and do not recognize its valuable purpose. When we lose our purpose of the human experience, we lose our joy. We no longer feel gratitude when we are in this frame of mind. "THIS is not OK," or "I am not OK" or "YOU are not OK" is a directive of conflict and dis-ease into the quantum field. That 'field' always delivers what you state. When you feel you 'have not,' then that is exactly what appears.

Unlimited realities exist within unlimited dimensions and within each are illusions of limitations. Each reality is reliant on the beliefs, thoughts and actions of the creator which means that he or she is 'right', yet we argue for one truth. Like ripples on water or the butterfly that flaps its wings that eventually contribute to a hurricane, the creator may not be aware that he or she is creating profound effects through even the most subtle thoughts and actions. The individual experience is so convincing that we rarely understand that it affects absolutely everything on some level. Choice is always in play.

Imagine a circle within a circle within a circle, non-ending. Each circle believes that it is its own isolated existence whose energy field ends at the perimeter. In actuality the ripples created within our circle do not stop at the seemingly defined wall that encompasses us. They continue outward and infiltrate all of the other circles. The individual views other circles as potential threats and strives to protect its boundaries, often blaming the other realities for interfering with theirs. In essence, they DO have a direct effect on ours because boundaries are illusions. We believe that what we create (or strive to create) is right and ultimate truth. Each circle of reality then imposes these truths on others. It is this illusion of separation that is at the root of conflict not recognizing that all truths are true. There is no one truth except that everything is ONE source. Humans confuse 'their reality' with 'reality.' Ultimate reality is all things, and all is true. The belief of each truth sends ripples throughout the endless circles, and can eventually cause a tidal wave. Yet, we only see the ripple. The individual holds incredible power, and each is equally important to the transformation of the illusion.

What is the individual journey? It is a perceived separateness. Our material world is designed to allow individual Oneness, but it is not the ultimate truth. Confused? It is the Oneness that we think is ME that is separate from everything. It is the "I am One and YOU are One" which is the belief that we are all separate. Thinking this makes it so. Because you believe you are One individual entity, it is created. The ONE makes it so because it desires to experience all facets of itself. We came here to know separation. That can only be done through unconsciousness. We came here to experience and then transform this unconscious state back to consciousness of our origins. This is what is taking place now on our planet. We individually get to conquer individual challenges.

Think about how very strange all of this is. We love our individualism. We protect it and think about nothing but ME, what I want and how I can get it. We fight for it, see others as either a facilitator or obstacle to our needs and actually kill one another to protect it. On the other hand, we spend our lives desiring the company of another. In fact, we believe that it is bad to be alone and that the 'single' person's objective certainly should be to find an 'other' to spend their life with and to produce 'other' individuals. We believe that happiness is to have the love of another, but more than half of us leave those relationships to find 'another' when that person doesn't fulfil the needs of the individual. We want to be with others, but on our terms. This 'individual' mind is always in conflict because we can never survive as individuals in a material world without one another.

You did not pop onto the planet on your own nor do you survive on your own. The individual is a perceived state of being. This is why we suffer as humans. We fight for our individual desires yet cannot survive as that individual. We do not celebrate the diversity of the collective and want the individual beliefs and desires to be that of all others. We are hypocrites, confused, and for the most part lost. This is by design.

The illusionary individual journey certainly is an amazing and mysterious one. Although we battle for our individualism, we know that the individual mindset is an unsatisfactory one. There are times when we feel alone and that there is no one 'out there' listening to us, helping us, saving us. It is then that we call out and pray to know that there are others that are with us, protecting and looking after us. It is that unseen world that we believe holds a saving quality. It is then that we find we don't really like being just ME on my own. We don't trust the 'others' within our own species for help. The ego then calls upon unknown powers to fix things.

Through our pandemic challenge, many learned how irritating it is to be with others, yet just how much we truly need one another. All of this is insane. We are completely confused about who and what we are. We have a love/hate relationship with ourselves.

Do you feel uncomfortable here? I refer to your presence on the planet. If so, you would not be alone. Many strongly feel that earth is not their home. They see the violence, distortions of our relationships with one another and selfish behavior that keeps us at odds and feel unsafe on a planet that has only one exit. Humans can be cruel beyond imagination, uncaring and willing to destroy their own habitat for personal gain. It is senseless and unexplainable. We are well aware that there are other options that come from giving, compassion and kindness yet the great majority do not take them. We are the creators of our own hell on a planet that offers heaven.

Who hasn't wondered what we are, how we got here and why? Who hasn't desired to know our individual purpose? Why am I here? Why do humans struggle so much? Why do we hurt one another? Why is there so much pain on the planet? We are lost. The human experience simply doesn't make sense. This is intentional.

Let us get some clarity on this subject of the individual journey. Simply put, it is the exploration of everything that we are not the essence of, but can be through the illusion experience. It is an exploration of pain and suffering which is a result of perceived individualism and separation. Through contrast we can understand the true power of love and unity. When one is in a dark hole, he or she simply cannot see the light. Perhaps it was the darkness that we became fascinated with because it is so foreign to our existence as light beings. It is like exploring quicksand. It looks quite harmless and safe. Although not totally stable, we do not anticipate its pull. Then, once you're in it, you are stuck and the more you resist, the faster you sink unless someone pulls you out.

There is a whole platoon of light keepers that have joined the earth experience who are here to give humanity a boost out of its pain. Humanity can only be pulled out, however, if it reaches out its hand. We must want it and that starts with knowing that a different state of being is not only possible but far surpasses fulfilling the ego's desires. Reaching out is that part of being human that gives us that choice that we seem so determined not to use in positive ways. Once we accept this guidance, we will know that we lose nothing through giving and that there is nothing to protect. This will take the human species into consciousness.

In the past, we recognized that we were humans with quantum powers and used them. Places such as Atlantis whether you believe is real or legend, demonstrated that amazing abilities used by dense humans can simply 'go wrong.' Atlantans in the spirit of being human went from utopia to using their powers for self-serving purposes. This is the human dilemma. It appears to be an addiction to lower frequency behavior. Once you go into that dark room, everything you view is dark and this is your reality. This is how most humans operate. I liken it to wearing sunglasses. If you don't know you are wearing them, you will see the world through those lenses. If you have rose colored glasses on, you will see the world as beautiful. Both are right. You are seeing the world exactly as the glasses project. You, however, put those glasses on and you can take them off. Mind you, I didn't say 'blinders.' I am referring to a view, beliefs, thoughts, and actions based on and prompted by that view. Of course, our choice of view is a little more complex than just switching out sunglasses. If only it were that easy!

Despite possessing unlimited powers of creation, humans gravitate to the dark side by choice to experience unconsciousness. It is that simple and when you grasp this, you can make any choice from this moment to break the chain of repeating pain. No challenge need take you into suffering which is the denial of circumstances. From darkness, darkness is taught and passed on until consciousness illuminates our condition. Consciousness is a choice which lights up the collective human energy field which in turn affects the choices of others. The abuser decides to stop. The addict seeks rehabilitation and on and on. Your higher choices prompt other higher choices without infringing on the free will of others.

Those less devious humans who function in ignorance are easily programmed by manipulative egos who understand their power and are motivated by their own fear-driven needs in what they believe is a limited material world. The ego is never satisfied. It seeks attention, power, and wealth that is a non-ending never-satisfied quest. Every area of our lives is affected by this behavior of self-service and false beliefs that have been passed on to each generation. Control is primary to its existence and this energy field has permeated our collective so deeply that most do not see past it. You may be participating in this behavior without recognizing it. Your judgment is more separation, even if you are judging that which you believe is 'wrong' or destructive. Judgement is disapproval. "You are not OK," is the statement that judgment makes. Anything that separates us is the ego in action and such choices do not shine light into the collective.

As programmed physical beings, we have trusted our eyes as the reporters of 'what is.' We conform to what is acceptable by the masses. Even children tease and torture other children who are 'different.' American youth is programmed through violent games and we are appalled when a child walks into a school with a weapon and randomly shoots. We name it 'wrong', yet the source of the brainwashing is not removed. In fact, adults are at the helm of the creation of this negative programming, devising new ways to amass fortunes through it. The same goes with our rampant illnesses. We are well aware that chemicals are sprayed on our foods. Then egos that earn off of the source of illnesses offer more remedies to 'fix' it with more poison, all because there is more money to be made. This is insanity. We are not born with these traits but learn them through the human shared energy field, our parents and their conditioning. This is a powerful density that permeates the planet and it takes a bold decision to step outside of the confined yet acceptable rules. We must establish a new foundation wherein the results are of a positive nature and not problems we create and then 'fix.'

Do you work for a business that causes destruction or illness? Choice is always yours to make. We live in a world that allows pollution and poisoning, makes efforts to clean it up, yet does not put an end to the source of it. We are not saying 'no' because the lazy ego is getting what it wants for the time being and society says it is OK. We are not rallying to close down anything that produces poison or illness. Instead, we buy it, eat it, and sell it.

The ego is not the source of our unhappiness. Our free will choices are. Those choices exist with or without the influence of ego. We cannot ignore our full ability to make a different choice. Our unhappiness is self-inflicted. Ego does not do this. WE choose to listen to the ego and abide by its endless needs. WE the ultimate power is choosing the path of unhappiness. The human experience is to go from light and all consciousness to darkness and unconsciousness until we have gathered as much knowledge as possible. We are in a cycle of duality.

Not all humans succumb to negative behavior, but all will certainly be challenged by it. That is part of the deal that allows us to evolve through choice. You won't know what that choice is until tested. Have you ever said, "I wouldn't have done that!" Perhaps you believe that you would choose ethics when presented with a challenge. It is easier to 'speak' ethics than to live them. Only when faced with that unpleasant event will you know where you rank in the matrix game. Humans who change the game by choosing divine power often deal with dire consequences. Those who buck the ego system have been chastised, ostracized and even killed. Empowered egos view enlightened humans as the most dangerous threat and great effort is made to demean and silence them. Through their peace and higher choices, destructive egos will go out of business. They will no longer be supported or believed. This does not take conflict or opposition it requires peace and action toward creating new foundation. Herein the meek shall inherit the earth.

Ego-ruled humans desire to keep 'good' or 'spiritual' people weak in our material world in order to maintain their status and control. 'Good' people are often easily lead to believe the many rules they must abide by. For example, receiving great wealth is usually labeled as evil and selfish by the religious community. To be 'good' is to be pious. Yet it is the masses, both spiritual and other, that fuel the wealthy who do not have the best interest of others in mind. This is free will choice that all humans must take responsibility for. We are taught that giving is good and receiving is 'wrong.' Have you ever read this in the bible? I am pretty sure that you won't. Last quote I heard 'it is just as easy to create a castle as a button,' and 'these things you shall do and more,' and 'ye are all gods.' Does that sound anything like 'receiving is evil?' Abundance is not judged. There is no lack. It is not wealth that spurs on bad behavior but the ego that uses it for self-service. No money or abundance is a problem. It can be had by all. Imagine a world wherein wealth is every human's state of being. It is possible even today. Imagine a world of giving and sharing, and teaching those in lack how they too hold the power and abilities to take care of themselves.

Spiritual people have held back from sharing their deepest thoughts and experiences in fear of being labeled crazy. Healers were burned and those who love and rally to protect nature are 'tree huggers.' Seeing the world in a positive light means that you have your 'head in the sand,' or are a Pollyanna. Making fun of light holders is the ego's favorite past time. It is safer to protect one's wellbeing through silence. Things are changing. We are stepping past the veils, speaking up and disregarding the consequences inflicted by the lower energies. And that is okay, because as Christ demonstrated, we are indestructible therefore nothing can truly threaten or harm us. This bold stand is a requirement for planetary advancement. Never forget that no matter the consequences of stepping outside of the matrix conditioning, no one can destroy anything or anyone. We are eternal. Our decisions in our human journey count, not some of the time, but all of the time. There is a dynamic, positive force emerging that cannot be stopped.

The human experience is neither good nor bad. Only the separate mind categorizes things and situations as good or bad, right or wrong. It cannot grasp the purpose. Yes, the human condition certainly appears to be bad, but it is a necessary experience to KNOW 'density' and to receive those 'tests' that all of us agreed to. What will you do when presented with them? Can you grasp the choice that every soul here made to experience whatever you judge as right or wrong? When we embrace our Oneness, the 'me' that is our constant concern dissolves along with fear. Service to the 'other' does not mean trying to 'fix' them because you decided that they need to be saved. Each person has the choice to ask and receive. When we respect that each of us has our own chosen path and teachings, accept this and offer assistance when the other party chooses to receive it, transformation occurs, and unity is restored.

So now that you are human, plopped on a planet that is floating in endless black space, dealing with other humans, what will you do with it all? Each of us inherently senses that we are not 'this' and is therefore quite uncomfortable with our disturbing circumstances. Some will explore the darkness and the ultimate contrast of Source. This is a huge challenge for others who seek peace and service to others because we must live with the consequences of the actions of others that are so often senseless and cruel. They are, however, not the problem but our best teachers. How can we effect positive change on a perfect planet? Here we are given opportunities. Without them there is no purpose in being human. Peace is simple to maintain on the top of a mountain in a monastery. It is truly tested when amongst those who oppose it and disrupt it. THIS is the true human challenge. Who are you as an awakened human when living amongst the pain that you cannot relate to? We can all maintain calm and tranquility until someone pushes our buttons. Peace and compassion are to be mastered.

A friend sent a quote to me by a Buddhist monk. It stated that the ultimate goal is to know ourselves and to choose our path and ending. There is no ending. There is no one path and there is no thing or 'self' to know. The essence of us is everything and that essence is expansion in all forms. You cannot 'know' that which you create in illusion. You simply make choices and experience it. My friend asked, "Don't you believe that Landria ends at some point?" My response is "No. Nothing begins nor ends, including the illusion of my persona." The person I know as 'Landria' is an expression of the one energy which is Source. Therefore, whatever

97

I 'do' with that illusion never ends. It becomes a part of the 'field' and the unending frequency choices within it. 'Landria' was a probability that always existed and always will. What I choose within this probability contributes to the direction of my next adventure. To know myself is to know that I am not Landria, but I am the creator of her. There are endless versions of her and endless paths that she chooses. That illusion is living out every probability and each choice made affects all of them. All exist simultaneously.

If we are perfection exploring all probabilities, why would we need teachings? If we are the source of all answers, knowledge, love, power, why would any 'learning' be necessary? While no one person can truly answer this question, there is a formula that it follows. As the all intelligence it explores. It experiences all of its forms. It demonstrates them. Since its creations are unlimited, this expansion has no limits or endings. It applies its powers without end. Have you ever wanted to do something grand such as climbing Mount Everest, run a marathon or any number of daring activities? There is always pain and frustration attached to such feats. What is the purpose? We seek a thrill. Fear makes us feel alive and generates great excitement. You can look at the mountain and imagine standing on the top of it or even BE on the top looking down, but climbing it to get to that peak in the most challenging of circumstances makes it so much more amazing. One feels the physical fatigue, can get injured, and even face the potential of death. It is only through this method can one know pain and triumph in a way perfection cannot. Even those who win Olympic gold medals usually go back again despite the hardships and challenges it presents. After all, what is to be done after you accomplish something great? We seek something greater. We believe that we want comfort, but the truth is that heaven can be boring. Look at how many wealthy, accomplished actors who have achieved goals beyond their dreams have ended up. Too often it doesn't seem to be enough. The challenge is what drives us. The expansion is the thrill. The fear drives us. The teachings are provided to the dense form of us that is ignorant so that the ultimate consciousness can know them. We are a part of the illusion of experiences and teachings. There are endless other uses of the power of the One beyond our understanding.

One of my students brought up a "Twilight Zone" episode to demonstrate this point. A man who loves gambling goes between big wins and losses. He chases women with varied success. He is either rolling high or low. This is, of course, a result of his choices and despite the 'lows,' he gains great satisfaction from the 'highs' which he feels are worth his choices. His life ends when he cannot pay back a loan shark and he finds himself on the 'other side.' He is shocked to see that he is standing at a casino table winning, beautiful women surround and want him, and everyone is cheering him on. This baffles him. How could he possibly have made it to heaven when he lived a life so destructive? Yet every night is the same. He constantly wins at the tables, every woman he desires adores him, and everyone loves him. He lacks for nothing. This goes on for a period of time until he becomes bored and unhappy. Gambling was no longer a game of risk with its highs and lows. The excitement of securing a beautiful woman's attention was gone since all of them desired him and he soon tired of them. In this heaven, there were no challenges and eventually he could not bear it anymore. He wanted out. It is at this point he realizes that he is not in heaven at all. He truly was in hell.

The decisions you make during your human experience have a massive impact ongoing. In other words, every human (and every other) role you have played and the choices you made is added to your personal energy field that impacts your next human or otherwise adventure. You will remain in the human experience until you master your pre-determined earth challenges. This applies to both long- and short-term, meaning that you can clear any karmic energy in THIS lifetime. Or you can come back.

Wouldn't you like to handle it all now? If you are not happy with the struggles of this lifetime, it can all come to an end, and I don't mean by sticking your head in a gas oven. I mean that you can make a decision. Everyone can end struggle now. It is what you came here to master. This is not possible outside of your human form. There is nothing to struggle against in that state of being. You can enjoy the human challenges. In fact, you will value them even more when you understand them and what they contribute.

Our matrix program is winding up, ready to transform into a 'slam bang finish.' It is not one event in time that happens for everyone. There is no universal clock ticking that imposes a time limit on when this happens. How and when you get there is your choice alone, neither right nor wrong. There are no mistakes, so don't beat yourself up for past decisions and their consequences. We exist in a holographic program and like Pacman, you keep coming back until you master the game. You don't quit Pacman the first time you get dissolved! That is the fun part – coming back and figuring it all out, to earn your name on the leader board. It is through repetition that we can change our responses to change our results. This is the entire exciting and challenging purpose. Don't miss it!

ONLY OPPORTUNITIES

Challenges are opportunities. Responses to them are choices. Those choices represent a frequency which then resonates with a corresponding reality. It determines everything that will happen in the next moment. Your choices and your frequency are everything. That is all you need to know. Simply put, the more compassionate response, placing 'service to others' first, is the frequency where you will experience love, compassion, bliss, and true power beyond your imagination. The closer you are to One, the more that expansiveness will be your reality.

Service to others is always a higher frequency choice because it aligns with unity and oneness which is closer to the Source of all things. This is the state wherein free will is no longer needed, as I shared earlier. We operate as one. Service to self, however, aligns with separation which explores the darkness of unconsciousness which is a lower frequency and further away from singularity. My guess is that you know a high frequency choice from a lower one. Placing another's needs first is not an easy task, but it is the individual choice that will change the game. In essence, you ARE serving yourself when you serve others because you are honoring unity which is shared. Whatever the 'other' receives, you receive. With the understanding of YOU and Source, being one thing, you know that what you do to another, you do to yourself. Therefore, your choice should be a simple one. Serve the 'other' well and you will experience equal if not greater rewards. One must not 'give' with the goal of receiving something, however. That would be an ego-based action motivated by self-service. Herein lies the true challenge and also the greatest opportunity. Everything is about your response. Everything. Your reality, the shared reality, cause and effect, all respond according to your beliefs and actions. The subject matter is irrelevant. Whether the challenge is fair or unfair, it is the response that counts. Was it one of compassion or ego-based? Unconditional love is the Source response. Unconditional. Love is unconditional. Ego is conditional.

In order to exist within the higher frequency dimension, we must always make the choice that places the 'other' first through compassion and love. We can make those 'service to others' choices even in the worst of times when it is most uncomfortable. As pure light beings there is no 'choice' to make. We simply 'are' that higher frequency in action. The individual experience is one of endless probabilities playing out just as it should. The matrix is designed to impose those challenges. It is not a punishment but opportunities within the game of endless probabilities. Higher frequency choices to those challenges can catapult one into awakening stardom and beyond! The more challenging the situation, the bigger the opportunity to get on the Matrix Leaderboard. So, think twice before you wish for an easy and uneventful life.

The universe and beyond is actively participating in our journey. It is affected by every choice. It is the pool of water undivided. Choice manifests unlimited conditions and results. Those results determine the progress of the whole. Are you ready to let go of your identity as a physical being and claim your unlimited power? If so, you can end suffering. If you are struggling with life, perhaps it is time to ask yourself why. When you know what you are, no form that you inhabit, nor events will ever present a threat. You will recognize the grand purpose of it all and your challenges will then hold value and the key to your evolution. This is faith. Faith is experiencing the pain of the play yet never letting go of a deep knowing that everything is always OK and always will be. Faith is the gateway to healing, peace and miracles. You are the participant and co-creator of miracles. They are not separate from you. You are that powerful and that magnificent, but only when you believe. It is the gateway to 'yes'. The quantum field always operates in 'yes.' It is abundant and IS the creative force that YOU are and create from.

So, when your relationship ends, your job ends, illness or loss hits, ask yourself what exists within this event. They are openings to new choices and the change that you experience is yours to direct. The cause of the situation was always operating 'with' you and your participation is required in order to experience it. It is the butterfly wing that resulted in a storm of which you are presented an opportunity for new creations and responses. Will you respond in faith and see the best in others, or will you allow your ego to battle what 'is' in order to get its way. Can you look deeper into the circumstances and find the opportunity to be great? If you do, then you truly understand your whole purpose here. It is not to gain a material comfort level but raise the frequency of the planet, one light being at a time. Your frequency. This must be your only concern.

THE PURPOSE OF FEAR

Fear is an experience unique to the human journey. I cannot say whether or not it is an emotion shared on other planets, but it makes sense that more advanced beings who understand their power would not share such a low frequency response. When one knows their powers of creation, they have no reason to experience fear because nothing can truly threaten them. They can manifest health and abundance at will knowing that they are the source of their creations, therefore there is nothing to protect. Humans are beginning to understand this but have much work to do. A deeper understanding that all situations are a result of our directives allows us to stop fearing. That which we fear we manifest.

Fear is the most dangerous of emotions. It causes us to turn on one another because it believes in lack and loss. Fear believes in defined endings, limitations and fights for power and control. But there is another side to fear which is why the human experience is so unique. There is often great satisfaction in fear. Why do people dangle from the tops of mountains, jump out of planes, hike through dangerous jungles, or jump off of bridges with only a bungee cord attached to their ankle? It is the thrill of coming close to our perceived impermanence, but not quite crossing that line. Of course, sometimes we DO cross it, yet many are willing to risk that possibility simply because no one truly believes that it will happen to them. Coming so close to danger is thrilling because it makes life so much more intense. We thrive on the thrill of fear.

Have you ever watched a scary movie, knew that it was not real, yet found yourself sleeping with the light on? Or perhaps you didn't let your foot dangle off the side of the bed like you usually do? We have all done that. I will be willing to bet that it didn't stop you from watching another scary movie. Fear can be our biggest motivator. Fear of poverty or loss can cause us to perform actions we would not consider if circumstances were comfortable. You may just go after that job you would never have considered, and an opening happens that takes you on a path of expansion. Fear spurs people to put themselves in life threatening situations when in fear of losing a loved one or even saving a stranger in harm's way. This is when one places service to others first because fear can momentarily obliterate the ego's self-concerns. Fear has its place in our world and adds to the exciting experience of the matrix.

To experience impermanence in the midst of infinity is one of the most unique feats of the ONE. This can only be accomplished if the human creation forgets its origins which is how fear entered the picture. Fear of the unknown, of the ending to life as we know it, of leaving the material world that we seek for satisfaction requires a memory wipe. Overcoming fear is the perceived return to power. I state 'perceived' because in truth we never left or lost it. Our power is indestructible and ever present. All human emotions such as anger, aggression, envy, greed, and judgments are simply a product of fear that the ego clings to because it believes in self-preservation, separation, and endings. We can never know these emotions when we understand that we are the conductor of the entire symphony, are the musicians, the instruments, and the music. Fear is addictive. We just can't seem to give it up even though it feels really bad! If we were to explain this to another life form, they might think that we were insane. In truth, we are.

A human journey without fear would take the fun out of it all. Facing fear is thrilling. It offers the excitement of triumph and glory. Have you ever seen people walking on hot coals at events? Despite their fear, they do it anyway. There is no thrill in having everything you want, receiving it with no effort, and living forever. There is no satisfaction or pride in that, nor gratitude when we finally achieve something that we worked so hard for. Fear serves a very positive purpose when used within the framework of positive change. It offers motivation and the reason to find solutions. Fear represents the alternative that we avoid which prompts action.

Think of it like the movie "Ground Hog Day" when Bill Murray lives the same day over and over. Even when he drives his truck over a cliff, he finds that nothing has changed. He wakes up the next day to live Ground Hog day over again. The thought of living forever depresses him until he comes to that wonderful space of acceptance and he makes the most of every day. The fear and expectations that caused disappointment are removed. It is then that the repetition ends, and he creates new beginnings. He truly begins to live his life in each moment.

The experience of fear is as 'real' as it gets in the material world. Imagine how wonderful it is to leave your body and experience total freedom, bliss and power without fear. You have experienced this unending bliss. It is your true state of being and you will experience it again soon enough. So, don't miss out on this contrast that allows you to know your bliss intimately. More important, don't miss out on breaking through this fear.

OBSERVATION NOT ELIMINATION

Fear rules this planet and its' woes. Fear is the ego, trained to find problems in everything in order to recognize potential threats to its' physical and emotional well-being. The ego is the survival mechanism within the lower frequency protecting personal desires. It is never satisfied with 'getting.' The ego protects this 'happiness' it seeks and will do anything to find or maintain it. Others are always a potential threat to its' goals. The result is that humans spend their lives seeking, always seeking, separating themselves from their true power and turning on one another. We have no tolerance nor acceptance of this journey. We struggle against one another, our lessons, and our entire way of life. We seek everything outside of ourselves. We are the beggar in the tattered robe whose pockets are filled with jewels, never reaching into those pockets. All of this is fear.

How do we move past all of this? How do we let go of the centuries of pain and suffering that is ingrained in every human? The answer is simple yet the most difficult to achieve. Let go. Of everything. When you LET GO you LET GOD. What does that mean? Let us explore further. Fear is not to be eliminated for reasons I stated. It is powerful, motivational, and exciting. Of course, it isn't so much fun when it wakes you up at 3:00 a.m. worrying about paying your bills or some other situation. So, let's take a closer look at how you can work with this fear and use it to your advantage. If you had no fear, you might not do anything about your money situation, lose your home and end up living on a park bench. Fear can motivate you to find a higher paying job, get new skills to secure that job, or any number of solutions. Fear of poor health can motivate you to eat healthier and start working out. It goes on and on. This is all highly beneficial when acted upon to find positive solutions.

The thing about fear is that it is based on having things a 'specific way' on its terms. Letting go of requirements to 'feel good' or safe, or happy, eliminates this urgent need and the negative feelings that come as a result. Fear is a part of the matrix journey, but can be used in the manner that can bring great satisfaction as I explained. So, the big question is 'how do we keep it in check?'

The key to overcoming fear is to observe it. When I first meet my students, most come with the habit of going into sheer anxiety and panic when their fears arise. They battle it. They don't want to experience fear. It simply feels bad and it seems to have a power all its own that the mind cannot override! When one believes the fears, it then transforms into a full-blown anxiety attack. When this happens, the ego is now in full control. We know that the ego battles everything that doesn't serve it. Like two separate personalities, the ego fights the negative feelings of fear, and neither can win. It is then that you have gone into full unconsciousness at its lowest level. There is an easier choice that you may not think would work, but is extremely effective. That is to go straight 'into' the fear. Watch it without engaging in it. You hear it, but you stop having a conversation with it. You stop envisioning its probabilities and simply 'feel' it without judging it. It simply 'is.' Fear is an emotion. It has no power until you engage in it and battle it as though a separate entity that you want to extinguish. See it as a catalyst to expansion. What is it telling you? "Here are your thoughts!"

Yes, fear are YOUR chosen thoughts, prompted by past triggers, beliefs and circumstances that YOU contributed to. Nothing just 'happens' in a moment. There are always choices along the way that brought you to that fearful moment. What were they? Can you change those patterns that placed you where you do not want to be? Are there triggers you are believing? Is the fear valid or is it a future event you are envisioning that never has to take place? This is your golden moment to stop battling fear and start listening to what it is telling you. Struggling against it is to deny that you have created it. What are the circumstances or patterns? What is the situation that can be turned around with a different choice? What are the actions, the thoughts, that will allow you to use fear to facilitate a new direction? Why are you struggling with it? Take a big step back and just look at it. Observe it. It is telling you a story that is one of limitless stories that you can choose.

There are different levels of fear. Have you ever dreaded an upcoming event or situation and your fear grew with each moment? Then the event arrives. Perhaps it's asking for a raise or giving a speech, the event is over, and you find out that it wasn't such a big deal after all. This is the kind of fear that may not serve a productive purpose. Worrying about losing your income and your home is a very real fear. Is it simply a probability that your fear is focused on? Yes. There are many other probabilities, but fear targets the most threatening ones. It is firing a warning shot that something must change. But most believe it and torture themselves with trying to 'make it go away.' Fear has no control over you. It is part of the human energy field that desires to shine the light on a new pathway. It is not the predictor of a defined future. Only you have full control over that. So, if you don't like the story that fear tells you. Change it and then make it real.

A practice that I teach is to go straight into fear. Look it right in the eye. What is it that you fear? Take a hard look and observe it. In other words, don't analyze it or try to figure out how to end it. Just examine it like you would a cut on your hand. It's there. It hurts. You don't need to have any 'thoughts' about it, try to figure out where it comes from or if what you fear will take place. Observe it. When you struggle against it, you are dousing it with fuel. So, okay, it hurts. It is unpleasant. It's an emotion. There is nothing to think about. It's there.

Fear can often be a giant in the room from which you run and hide. It is so massive that you cannot escape it. It is so big and daunting that you feel you have no chance against it. So, it sits there, looming over you. It is time to come out from under the bed and face the giant. He is not there to harm you. He will simply tell you about the probability that you are focused on. That is all. He is your voice and your story. There is only one person in charge of that story. You. Reality is a choice. Your story is a choice. Your story creates your reality.

The next step you can take is to ask yourself how you can change the situation that is prompting your fear. Taking action toward positive change is one of the most powerful things you can do because it is a directive waiting to kick into action. Solutions are the probabilities that fear is not showcasing. It is not designed to be positive. It is designed to find the worst-case scenarios. Even though you may be entrenched in fear, you can easily avert your attention to other probabilities by making a decision to seek them. By 'seeking' solutions, you prompt answers from within the quantum field which judges nothing and always has your highest and best interests in mind. Solutions and answers are always there, but fear has caused your attention to be placed on everything but that which could affect great and positive change. Fear, remember, is a catalyst to positive change if you choose that path. It is only a beacon warning you of what YOU are focused on and can redirect. It is then that opportunities you never imagined will appear. The right people, an offer, an opportunity, a contest win, or anything can suddenly materialize. There is no trick to doing this. Any effort to change your situation and 'seeking' will lead you to answers. Fear and worry do not allow for such openings. Is it time to stop believing the stories that fear tells you? You are bigger than fear because you created it.

While thoughts are things, you may be concerned that if you take fear head on and give it attention, you will manifest more of what you fear. This is not the case. Battling negative feelings creates a much more negative and powerful manifestation of what you fear because fighting it doesn't make it go away, right? It just amplifies what you fear. The observation of it and not 'fearing fear' sends a positive message into the quantum field of 'here it is again – my human emotion – I will just sit with it.' That's it. You aren't doing anything with it. You observe it without allowing it to control you. You feel it without struggling against it. Therefore, instead of becoming upset because you 'believe' the fear, you observe it without an opinion. The universe always says 'yes.' If fear is there, observe it and you will find that it will begin to dissolve.

Our usual response is to struggle with the thoughts that are creating the fear and anxiety. Believing the fear, struggling against it and fearing its' story makes it real. That message is 'I believe this story and that is why I fear.' What you believe is what you manifest. When you master observing fear and no longer engage in it, it eventually it becomes an annoying whining child in the room. When you aren't reacting to it, it eventually stops. Observing the fear is not believing it, but experiencing it. You will feel it, but you no longer have thoughts about it or go into analyzing it. This is a technique I use with students with physical pain. I have them focus on the pain! And guess what happens. In every case, the pain lessened, and in some instances completely disappeared. When they looked at it head on, they were actually taking charge of the fear and accepting the situation. They stopped running from it, turned around and looked directly at it.

Fear raises your blood pressure, gets your nerve endings riled up, and causes illness. When you accept that it will be with you throughout your life and you know that you can use it in profound and positive ways, it is no longer a problem. When it appears, you use it as a messenger that something must change in your life and is an opportunity for expansion. What are those steps you can take? What life changes would shift that fear and take you into a new, wonderful reality? Ask yourself what that message is and what opportunity is presenting itself? If it is money and you take action to improve your situation, your fear will dissolve. You will feel in control from a positive, creator perspective. It is that simple.

There are other fears that my students have presented that are fabricated. In other words, they have fear based on a story they create in their head. Granted, this comes from conditioning, perhaps a traumatic event, or the programming from others. No matter the reason, the fear is still a choice. It can be believed and battled or observed. The source of it is irrelevant at that point. The response is what fuels it or uses it to your advantage.

Next time you experience fear, use these simple steps and you may find that shifting out of it is much easier than you imagined. You will feel empowered and in control, not from an ego standpoint, but as a powerful being that has choice who no longer chooses struggle. You are capable of so much more than you may imagine. When presented with challenges, you will know this. Do not underestimate your powers of change. Circumstances are always the pathway to something greater and those that appear to be negative are not happening 'to you' but for you. Go ahead and feel fear. It is a reminder that something big is about to happen for you and that your decisions will take you to it. Focus on that next big thing that awaits you and get excited!

THE ESSENCE OF EGO

The ultimate conclusion to this seemingly insane ride, is to master the dense vibrational form – to raise the frequency within density and transform back into light. This challenge is presented by the human body, which is purposely designed to be heavy and slow, dense and difficult. Its low vibration shrouds the power that drives it which creates a perfect home for the accompanying ego. The ego is the energy field that resonates with the heavy body and takes center stage in its role as the ultimate separation experiment. It is rooted in the material world, specializes in self-service, lack, power and endings. It is the cloak that disguises the light that created it.

Even forgiveness is actually a part of the ego's energy field. While humans think of forgiveness as a good thing, which certainly is a great start, ego is still in control in that equation. It is the most challenging of the One's tests because it epitomizes the human belief that there is 'another' separate from it and that the 'other' is wrong and has somehow damaged it. It believes that it must 'forgive' that which has inflicted wrongdoing according to its rules of right and wrong. The ego holds others accountable for sins that it deems unnecessary and that its 'awakening' allows it to release that 'wrong' doing. The ego frees itself from deep anger, rage, hurt and resentment through forgiveness. So, you see, it is still a product of the ego because the belief in separation caused it to have to forgive in the first place. It is not truly free. The ultimate release is to recognize that there are no mistakes, no right, nor wrong. The One doesn't make mistakes. Everything is intentional, choice and opportunities. Some are simply more challenging than others. Enlightened ones do not require forgiveness. They recognize all as purposeful, intentional, choices and opportunities.

To blame is to judge which is the lowest of frequencies. That is why forgiveness is still not totally letting go because it labels right and wrong with no benefits. Total enlightenment encompasses the understanding that everything is exactly as it should be and that all 'sins' are a product of fear, pain, and the cycle of it that has been passed down. Fear strikes out against others. Is that wrong or is this an opportunity for compassion? Which response will heal and break the cycle of judgement, right and wrong? I think you know.

The highest form of forgiveness is the realization that no one can truly make a mistake because there is no chaos in the universe, and these 'wrongs' are gifts in the form of tests that you have agreed to play out. In other words, forgiveness is not necessary. The power of forgiveness through the eyes of the ego extends to yourself and your own actions. How often do we regret our past actions and 'hate ourselves' for them because we have done something 'wrong?' There is neither right nor wrong. You are learning and waking up. Your 'mistakes' allow you to know the pain of lower frequency choices. How can that be wrong? No one can know right unless wrong is experienced. That 'other' that wronged you is also a part of the big plan and intentional learning. What you did 'wrong' needs no forgiveness either. You are a babe in very deep, dark woods. We fall and skin our knees before we can walk with stability and eventually run. Is that wrong? It is learning and does not need forgiveness. Embrace that. Would you not also desire to be loved despite your wrongdoings? The other is all part of the divine experience and there are no true mistakes. We must give that which we would want to receive no matter what the 'other' has chosen. Through this we learn and return to light.

The ego is never totally happy because its desires can never be completely obtained. This is because its job is to always get more. More is a goal that can never be reached, therefore 'more' always exists within the ego's mission. This is demonstrated with the movie star whose adoration no longer fulfills, whose last award must be followed by another, whose beauty is fought to maintain. The wealthy very often tire of their riches and more is needed. This is, of course, not the case with all rich and famous, but those who seek the wealth and to be famous to fulfill their ego's needs certainly qualify. Just look at the lottery winner statistics of bankruptcy and divorces. It appears that the 'more' that the ego seeks does not solve its problems nor quench its thirst. This is why the ego must dissolve or at least take a back seat in order to end the mission of 'more.'

The ego in its power may congregate with other egos whom support its own cause provided those egos are in alignment with it at all times. Otherwise, the ego can easily turn on its fellow egos in a moment. It believes in 'good,' 'bad,' 'right,' and 'wrong' according to its own rules. It is fickle and will eliminate other egos even if they support it, if there is an advantage to gain in the material world. This is common place in politics and criminal rings. The ego is the veil that allows us to know emptiness, darkness, and loneliness; especially loneliness because even other egos are its worst enemy. It cannot find unity even within itself. Are you a part of a 'group' that opposes another? Or are you a part of a group that provides solutions and enacts positive change without making others 'wrong?'

This human experience is a small blip on the radar screen of your expansion and an exciting one if you embrace it. You can have amazing fun with this privileged position that you chose. There is a good chance that you haven't even scratched the surface of your capabilities because one thing alone stops you – you are listening to the ego mind. From this self-limiting energy comes fear of losing control which then triggers preservation of the self that in turn brings great unhappiness. From there, we can easily spiral downward to another place of human fabrication - hell. Hell is very real within the illusion. When we step outside of the matrix, it does not exist. It was yet another experience through an explored frequency of 'me.'

Humans have one goal – happiness. Operating strictly from ego, we go after this in two primary ways - acquiring things and desired situations. Most dedicate a lifetime to these pursuits, usually never achieving them to any real satisfaction and despite centuries of this unsuccessful formula, continue to repeat it. The ego simply does not know its options. Happiness is a moving target and a constant future goal that comes with consequences, yet this does not deter the ego. Just look at our prisons and the stories within their walls.

Like fear, the ego has positive attributes. It protects the human body and its needs. It can also protect its desires to serve itself as we have discussed. Observed, it does not have to rule in the extreme negative. We can know its directives and assess its intentions without acting upon them. Your higher self always has the power to override the self-serving thoughts of the ego and take action accordingly. Again, the whining child will eventually stop no matter how annoying it is. One must be in a state of consciousness to make higher choices. Awareness is critical. This takes practice. Once again, observation becomes a powerful tool.

THERE IS NO BATTLE OF EVIL AND GOOD

The battle between evil and good is as real as two little children playing war with plastic army men. We see perfect children acting out earthly horrors that they have been taught. The child in that moment feels the power of the battle and with some sound effects can destroy an entire platoon. There is no thought in what the game represents or the consequences. After all, they are plastic toys. What damage could such a simple game inflict? Plenty. We are all creators of both evil and good within our game. Each are a choice. Like the children playing, we agree to the creation of both sides. Without it, there is no game, nothing to conquer. Someone has to be 'the bad guy' to keep the conflict and challenges going. Without 'the bad guy' there cannot be 'the good guy.' Duality keeps the entire multi-verse of illusions acting out choice and challenges, triumph and defeat. If this is difficult for you to believe, then you are simply deep in the mind of ego, separation, limitations, and a state of fear. There is no situation that has to bring us to annihilation of one another. There is another way.

There is a balance within the matrix of this 'good and evil' in order for the game to work. When 'evil' appears to overpower our planet, light beings are injected to even out the playing field. There is fairness in this game and there are winners, but only in the illusion. One cannot 'win' over oneself in the bigger picture. There are conclusions to this game at which time the players move on to new challenges and experiences. There are other games where planets have been decimated and abandoned. Great feats of heroism and community have been achieved in such scenarios.

Earth has been part of this cycle of 'losing' but is now positioned to win. This balance exists throughout the universe. The frequency of these games fluctuates. In other words, a balance of positive and negative may exist on a higher frequency eliminating the destruction and separation that Earth experiences. The winning and losing may not function on the deep level that we know here with its extreme highs and lows.

It is true that the influence of light beings and the awakening of dense ones can 'tip' our collective toward light. It is said that it only takes 100 million awakened beings in order to catapult our planet into a golden era of peace. Whether that number is accurate or not, no one truly knows. However, it is true that a majority of humans is not required to awaken the planet's race because light is more powerful than darkness. One cannot bring darkness into a room of light. A dark room, however, is lit whether with a match or a spot light. Light holds all power and darkness provides opportunities. One cannot know light without darkness.

That unknown, unseen world is frightening to us because we don't believe that we control it. In true human form, we see it as something separate that has its own agenda. The ego loves to protect itself from 'that out there,' believing that it can do this by controlling the material world and others in it. Control is an illusion that perpetuates conflict. It views that unseen world as something evil that is 'out to get us.' This is conditioning that has been used to keep us in disempowerment. This belief has filled movie theaters and it sells. We claim we despise evil, yet it permeates our entire existence here, fueled willingly with our attention. Ask anyone if they watch the news, especially if it is tragic or frightening. It is the predominate choice for information. Bad news is addictive, and fear is what we are used to. Ironically, that 'evil' is us. We are not watching another. We are watching ourselves. As One energy, evil surely is Source also.

This is an adventure unlike any other and you are here in this fabulous, torturous, beautiful, amazing and insane hologram by choice. What were you thinking? Well, you're here now so you might as well make the best of it all. It will pay off big time if you do. You will understand just how incredible this journey is once you leave, but my wishes are that you grasp that before you do. It will enhance your visit that much more and accelerate your expansion both here and beyond your physical existence. What you do here counts because you carry it with you when you leave. Because of our collective connection, your spiritual evolution accelerates others. So, never doubt that you have a profound purpose. Whatever you are going through, when you make higher, loving choices, it will all be worth it.

WHAT ABOUT REINCARNATION?

Reincarnation is a big subject with many theories and opinions. However, I will address how it fits into your human experience from a science perspective because it is actually quite simple. You, that body that you see in the mirror, is a container for a role that you play. It is all part of the 'game' that allows you to be a seemingly limited human. Since energy cannot be created nor destroyed, and everything is energy, you are NOT that body and therefore must have been and will be many other things. The actor does not star in one movie or play. He or she plays many roles in many plays. The more experienced, the more proficient he/she becomes as an actor and will choose more challenging roles. It is then that 'by popular demand' they are able to take on more expansive roles.

Energy is infinite and ever expanding, thus no human is stagnant. Your body changes, your thoughts and experiences, all continue to evolve. Being human on planet Earth is just one stop you have made along the way of possibly hundreds or even thousands of human lives. Not all humans have been here before, but they are few. Most of those beings volunteered to raise the planet frequency and come from advanced realms. They too must abide by Earth's matrix rules. Like Christ, their mission is to demonstrate that everyone is capable of overcoming all challenges within the illusion.

You most likely do not remember any of your past lives and this is deliberate. The brain can only process and deal with one life experience at a time. Know that just because you don't remember your past lives does not mean you weren't here before. Learning and achieving your spiritual goals on such a dense planet cannot happen in one lifetime. Humans who have mastered the Earth matrix have chosen many scenarios. If you chose to master forgiveness and did not conquer it, you will come back in various human roles until that is achieved. You may then choose to master an illness, or the challenges of taking care of someone else who is ill. Perhaps you desire to know great wealth and power, testing what you will do with it. The choices go on and on. Think of this as a spiritual university. You, the one person you believe that you are, cannot go through every class and graduate, in one visit. Each class represents a different role, a different life, like one semester in college. You get to improve with your return visits and take on new roles that contribute toward your degree.

Your continuing roles contribute to the transformation and progress of your energy field through the human facade. Upon being presented with what may seem to be very unfair treatment by others, you may spend many years working on forgiveness or perhaps countless lifetimes! Your next class may be to know and be another culture, religion or skin color. What would it be like to walk in the shoes of the people you may be judging in this life? You will get to know that soon enough because when you do not master the class, you have to take it over. It will be presented in a different manner that can drive home the point. Did you look down on homeless people and did not choose compassion? There is nothing more effective than coming back as a homeless person, to know the truth that compassion could have been a life altering choice for that man or woman you passed by.

If you are having difficulty opening up to the idea of reincarnation, perhaps you will want to explore the amazing discoveries of children who have detailed memories of past lives. These children have known their former names, details of their death, street addresses, family members, and scenarios that are impossible for them to have made up. This has been documented long before anyone could do a Google search online to get information. Are those dreams or made up stories? I think neither. These young people simply have a thinner veil between their human form and the quantum field. Youth has a higher vibration and cleaner slate, allowing them access to such information. This is why children often see 'ghosts' and later in life usually lose these capabilities. The veil thickens as they are exposed to the density and programming of humanity. Do you relate to a former life? Perhaps you have repetitive dreams as another person. Pay attention to these.

Energy has unlimited frequencies and vibrations. The more traumatic the death, the more likely you will bring the feelings or memory of that trauma with you. I have experienced such memories myself and recollect the final moments of a past life. That 'field' of all intelligence, all-knowing and all creation is not separate, and anyone can access it, however, it is not necessary. One can work through any 'past life' trauma now. Having memories of a former life can interfere with a present life which is why few of us remember them. It is best not to carry the physical memories of past traumas. Each of us already carries the energy field that was created by them. Details are not necessary. While past life regression can sometimes bring positive benefits through understanding and release to those who have carried this trauma forward, everyone can release such energy in this lifetime without a formal hypnotic regression. All too often, I see students clinging to that former identity to solve today's problems. This is the ego needing answers. All 'karma' can be resolved in this lifetime regardless of your past. Yes, even if you were a serial killer. There is no judgment in the field of energy – only choices and frequencies that determine the next experience. Perhaps you save animals in this life or are a caretaker. This is powerful.

Earth is the most challenging of the planets in the universe because it takes the essence of our origins which is total peace and love, to a place of great pain and isolation that is foreign to us. So, congratulations on choosing such an intense adventure. No matter what your chosen mission was upon re-entry, rest assured that you can accomplish much in a place that takes you to extreme challenges if you understand that they are presented for your evolution and not to be avoided. Avoiding and denying them is what keeps you in the karmic return to Earth. Floating around as a light body cannot possibly allow you to KNOW what fear is, or pain, or anger. You can have it explained all day, but it isn't until you enter a dense body, forget all that you have been, and believe that you are limited that you can know extreme contrast.

Now let's address those 'first timers.' A small group of people are here on their first visit with a specific mission outside of personal spiritual evolution. This is because Earth has hit a critical tipping point and linear time is of the essence. Planet Earth can no longer sustain the abuse and careless actions inflicted by its irresponsible inhabitants. Humans are not only abusing the planet, but one another and the innocent other inhabitants such as plants and animals of whom are rarely valued as the gifts they are. We spray chemicals on them, torture and use them for testing, and eat them without gratitude. Because WE are ONE, ALL other God expressions are affected by our actions here and the lack of progress by the human species has presented a universal dilemma. An intervention was necessary in order to maintain the cosmic balance of the universe. Our ego-driven actions have caused alarm to our cosmic neighbors whom are greatly affected, and it was decided that a 'remedy' of a non-controlling manner was the best possible course of action. This was implemented by placing reinforcements of a more advanced nature into the mix. These beings agreed to participate in this planetary game, with the goal of raising the frequency. This provided a 'boost' to the collective without interference. This positive influence does not infringe on free will but is an opportunity for humans to see a way out of the darkness and make higher individual choices. It is like going into a cafe that sells coffee and suddenly tea is also on the menu. But unlike coffee and tea, our choices are much more radically different and impactful.

The high frequency influence is here, active and walking amongst humans in indistinguishable roles. It could be the homeless man or the wise neighbor. Not all are obvious. These light beings have a clear assignment and karma is not a part of their energy field. That being said, they too will know the 'human experience' and will deal with the same challenges. Such change makers do not have children nor strong material ties to Earth. You won't find them hoarding or attached to strong opinions nor opposition. Children, a spouse, political, religious or corporate entrenchment are all distractions from their purpose. They may dabble in such areas, but will detach and move onto their mission. You may know someone like this. They have a deep understanding of the spiritual realms that are unexplainable to most but come naturally to them. They also have knowledge of the universe that they generally do not share with others who cannot comprehend what may seem like insane concepts and ideas. They 'know' things and have a natural ability to communicate with the higher realms so as to share such information with the denser energy fields. They were the 'different' ones in the family that did not seem to fit in.

There is an even a smaller group that has never been here in human form and whose mission is also to participate in the transition of the planet simply by being a positive 'presence.' They may never teach or be engaged in society. Their energy field alone contributes to the positive tipping point. They have experienced challenges on other planets in other forms and in dimensions where neither planets nor physical bodies exist. They too have chosen the accelerated challenges of the material world that

124

'forgot' what it was by design. They usually do not know why they are here nor engage in any kind of 'stance' that is of a negative nature. Most live a peaceful and compassionate life which is all that is needed. Very few will know them nor will they demonstrate notable accomplishments. Can you open your mind to this, or will you remain in the dense box of limitations that we have lived in for centuries? Do you have any limits in your beliefs about what is possible? The ONE has no limits, therefore, why would you?

Much of what you feel is directly related to your past lives, your relationships with people whom you have known before and the present influences. That energy that you created in the past (there is no such thing as time, but let us use this term for better understanding) comes with you. It is not something that you leave behind. That is impossible. As there is no such thing as time, that energy field you have created through your choices is affecting you now. A random incident may trigger positive or negative feelings for no apparent reason. Your personality may be different from your family with no real explanation, such as low self-esteem or anxiety when you have been brought up in a totally positive environment. This is karma. It is not something that you shake off when you die. Karma is simply the frequency that you chose when tested in your past journeys and if not higher ones, you will return to do better. Many people have released this karmic energy simply by letting go of everything. Letting go of anger, blame, fear and expectations requires no replay. It just dissolves. In fact, karma is no longer necessary for anyone to carry forward as long as you stop focusing on YOU and what YOU do or do not get. This places you in a higher intention that is not about the ME in the dense world, but the energy field of the ALL. When you go into this space, lessons are no longer required. Awakening dissolves them as you 'get it' and connect your physical self with your higher self. They no longer battle one another. Your attention is then toward the

ONE, the good of ALL which actually brings healing, abundance, joy and peace that is not possible when you are ME focused.

Now let us talk about all of those other people you were entangled with along the way. Have you ever felt as though there was a strong connection to someone that you can't quite put your finger on? It may be a perfect stranger. This is real. I am not referring to love interests but all people from those whom are close to you to the random stranger you meet. These connections include that person that irritates you most, the nasty boss or overly protective parent, or even a challenging personality that constantly shows up in your life. These are the most valuable of relationships and serve as master teachers. Perhaps the past life wherein you were selfish has recreated itself into a scenario placing you as the disadvantaged one and a relative is holding back on helping you. That annoying person at the office that really gets under your skin is your opportunity to see past their pain and offer compassion no matter how difficult it may be. These lessons continue to play out. All of us have experienced feelings of another. Maybe you don't even know it. Perhaps you just have 'a bad feeling' or inspiration, or an idea. All of this is part of your shared energy field communicating with you not only from those you have a karmic connection to but everyone. This is why it is so important to clear out the lower energies that you are hanging onto. Awakening is impossible until you do so. Karmic debts can be paid now simply by releasing the negativity you may hold for another. Letting go is actually your biggest test. Time to graduate, don't you think?

Here is a consideration for you that I won't elaborate on, but want to give you something else to ponder. Have you ever had feelings, dreams or recollections of being another person at another time? That life you may have thoughts and feelings about which existed before this human expression may not have been 'you' in another life. This bigger subject I am referring to is the fact that ALL is ONE and therefore, ALL humans ultimately experience EVERYTHING. That person that you despise is you. The homeless drug addict is you. Every human who has ever lived and ever will exist is essentially you. Any and all experiences of 'another' are ultimately yours, even if you personally did not choose that physical form. Let us address all of those people who claim to have been Cleopatra or Marilyn Monroe, or some other famous person. It is not so far-fetched that this is totally possible. In fact, we all were these people. Yes, I know that is an 'out there' statement, but if all is ONE, and time actually does not exist, then it must be true. If all is ONE, then the ONE is experiencing it all as ONE. There wasn't a separate Cleopatra. We all experienced being Cleopatra.

Believing YOU are ONLY YOU, that human you identify with, is a limiting human thought. That thought is in alignment with our entire dense, limiting ways that have kept us living under a rock and denying all that we are. All of your feelings and actions are directly influenced by the ONE energy and why it is crucial for you to treat all humans as you would treat yourself. Isn't this what we are told as children? So quickly we resort to thinking that we know better and the separation and judgement begins. This is the critical purpose of all existences – to know that we are One and to operate on that loving, caring, non-judgmental level.

Now let us talk about what happens between when we transition. Yes, a life review is required. It is the only way that we can examine our performance as students and know how we can do better next time. That ONENESS that I speak of kicks in and upon your life review you will clearly understand that that 'other' is not an 'other' but now YOU. This is how we experience the feelings of 'the other' of whom we may have offered our compassion or perhaps our criticism. As I explained, the ONE of which we are is experienced by you not as YOU the human but by ALL. It is not just a one-sided review. YOU become both perpetrator AND victim. We then know the effects of our actions to OURSELVES. Is that too much to comprehend? If you find this interesting, stay tuned for my next publication. We will go further 'out' into that space that is so unknown to us.

Human or not, if you believe that you are just Bob or Sally or David, then what happens when you die? It is impossible for you to never exist in some other form. Therefore, you have the choice to reincarnate in order to continue your expansion into all knowledge through experiences. Not all reincarnations are in human form. Why would they be? Perhaps you desire to know what it is like to fly. What about a plant? What would that be like? They are alive like everything else. All is energy and energy is intelligence. WHAT we choose to experience next has nothing to do with being human so much as just a new exploration. That is what the ONE does. Beyond the contrast of what it can be, we cannot know. We don't need to know. Humans are designed that way. We are supposed to be ignorant. THAT is an experience in itself.

So, do you believe that YOU were nothing before this human form? Do you believe that YOUR energy is destroyed upon your death? There are far too many experiments that would prove that is impossible. However, if you believe that then you will create and exist in that reality at least for some time. You may experience hell or blank nothingness. It is the illusion of your creation and beliefs. There is nothing wrong with that other than it really is a bit limiting, don't you think?

In conclusion, whether you are a believer of our Oneness or not, think about reincarnation for a moment. It is simply energy morphing, transforming, and recreating itself. That is all that it does. All of it is purposeful, therefore intelligent beyond human comprehension. It is the endless expansion of all forms and the nothingness. It is all things at all times. Therefore, you must have been something else. The ONE expanded into endless expressions and the key ingredient to knowing this is space. Space is a part of the ONE which allows us to appear separate. Never forget that the space between you and I is US also and you are always communicating with it. It is the ultimate intelligence and if it ever collapses, we shall then return to that ONE point of all things at all times without the expansive expression that you know now. We shall return at that point to our ONE form, the pinpoint of existence of which scientists believe the 'big bang' came from. For now, WE want to explore everything else.

I don't know about you, but I find great comfort in knowing that there is another journey in store. Perhaps you would prefer not to come back to this planet. After all, it is the most challenging in our universe. It is also the biggest opportunity for evolution and expansion that can move you up in the frequency scale. What is that? A lower frequency is what dominates earth humans and a higher one takes us into our light being, joy, peace, and recognizing no limitations. In other words, the higher frequency takes us closer to what we came from, pre-illusion. The choice to raise our frequency is the exploration of more and more and more that goes beyond alien life, angelic beings and even archangels. Our ability to raise our frequency is unending. The ONE is unending. So, won't you do your best here? It is hardly a blip on the radar screen and soon you will be off to transformation. That will depend on what you accomplish here. The game is to achieve the highest frequency as a human which is a big feat considering the density we took on. There are big rewards for doing so. We have devised our own prize for achievements.

WHY WE SUFFER

Suffering. That word holds power. It almost hurts to hear it because it is a word every human can relate to and has experienced. It begins when we are babies, expressing or sometimes demanding our needs and even our wants. We cry and scream and suffer. No one avoids suffering. What is suffering and why do we continue to experience it? Let me remind you again, of our human basics. We create everything therefore, we create suffering. Yes, we create the very thing we seek to escape but don't seem to have the ability to end. We create the ignorance that we stepped into and we create its perpetuation. Let us explore further.

Suffering is a result of non-acceptance of circumstances, of self-created negative thoughts about those circumstances, of believing the fear that we conjure. It isn't the pain we experience but the non-acceptance of that situation that creates the suffering. Suffering is the internal statement "this shouldn't be this way, this is wrong" or "things should be different," or "this holds no purpose, it is unfair and doesn't make sense." These are stories that we alone create which although affects others, formulates our own reality and no one else's. The pain of circumstances escalates into suffering when we continue to battle all that the ego does not want to participate in. This is the state of ego which does not like anything that gets in the way of its goal to feel good and lack nothing. Those goals include how it thinks others and the world should behave to please it.

Suffering encompasses blame, victimization, judgement, unfairness, fear, and the belief that we do not control our circumstances or the cause of them. We believe that something is 'happening to us' that is generated by an outside source or person(s) independent of us. They are the problem. Their decisions are causing my pain and suffering. If only the government, or my employer, or my spouse would stop inflicting pain on me, then everything would be OK. This is suffering. The stories shift cause and responsibilities to 'the other.'

Pain is at the core of the human experience. It comes in the form of sadness, anger, depression, hopelessness, feelings of loss and despair. All of these emotions are precious gifts when one recognizes that they contribute to the illusion experience and our collection of knowledge. We didn't come here to eat sweets and to lounge on the beach. We came here for the tough stuff. To battle these emotions creates suffering which takes pain to a whole new level. Suffering occurs when we don't accept pain as a positive opportunity to evolve. We simply want pain to 'go away.' Suffering is when we are in service to self that wants nothing to do with challenges. It wants everything and everyone to change in order to establish its desired emotional and material state. Pain does not have to control you. With practice, it can be accepted and observed. Although observation does not eliminate pain, it lessens its intensity because you no longer battle it. It is then that you can observe your own reactions and thoughts, and make new choices. Observation allows you to view the experience instead of immersing yourself in the emotions. Perhaps it is time to adopt a new story to your pain that can dissolve it.

Suffering is 100% ego-based thinking that is only in service to self. This includes wanting others to be different even if you want the 'best' for them. You might say "No! I am in service to others. I suffer because I don't want to see others in pain or their own suffering. I want the best for THEM!" This is ego. By not accepting the journey and challenges of others, you are wanting things, actions or circumstances of others to be a certain way for YOU. YOU will feel better when THEIR circumstances change according to your rules or beliefs. Even when you want the best for others, suffering is when you do not accept that their pain is intentional and purposeful. This may seem especially cruel to believe that a hungry or abused child participates in such pain by choice and that we should accept it. Acceptance is not approval nor 'non-action.' Your purpose is to come to the aid of others and to facilitate positive change by providing options and shifting any judgement to compassion. That is not an infringement on free will. However, when you understand that the child and other players agreed to engage in their scenario in order for them and others to evolve, you can see it differently. You can end contribute to the end of all suffering of others through facilitating solutions, acceptance and love. You will then step into the role as a changemaker without 'requirements' of the outcome. You simply offer aid and assistance and accept that everything is exactly as it should be because WE are directing all of those circumstances and outcomes. These are your opportunities. Feed the hungry, give comfort to the homeless, remove the abused child from its circumstances, rescue the animal. Unless the players in these scenarios do not desire your assistance, giving and service to others without judgment is powerful.

Accepting that every human on this planet chose challenges that result in pain to master the game of density, allows us to end suffering. It is like being at a university. Some classmates choose complex physics and others choose basic math. No one looks at the more challenged students as 'wrong' nor do we try to get them to quit. They WANT to experience complex physics because they desire to become masters at the craft they chose. Life paths are no different. One might have chosen illness or to be physically disabled. Another chose poverty or abuse. We cannot know the journey that brought them to this place in their spiritual adventures. The very person that abuses them may have been the abused in a prior life. Switching roles allows each to KNOW that experience and to also make their own free will choices to resolve pain and 'do it better' this time. No one can know another's path, but can end suffering by simply accepting it, and becoming the catalyst for their positive choices by offering another way. This must be done without expectations.

I want to remind you that the corrupt, angry adult is an equal light being to the innocent child. We are not the vulnerable form you see that plays out its chosen position. We only appear weak in a material world and are an accumulation of our choices reflected within our human persona. This is superficial because we essentially are equal, all knowing, powerful beings. That 'person' you see and evaluate based on their appearance and responses is an unending energy field that may have been the prince, the pauper, the prophet, the leper, the warrior and exist in eternity. There is no age to us. You too were a child and have evolved into something else. So, what are you and what will you be? It is unending, no matter what form you take. The human you are is evolving at every moment. So, who and what are we? We are one in the same. Do not let the façade of the human form fool you. It is a catalyst for powerful choices which motivates us to end suffering. One may not be inclined to assist the dirty, homeless alcoholic as readily as the innocent child, but they are equal in every aspect. Only judgement separates us and dictates our actions according to those beliefs. These are not easy decisions to make but I assure you that when we leave these heavy bodies, we are all equally loved and powerful light beings that continue in our choice of experiences. The dirty alcoholic deserves equal love and assistance as the innocent child. In fact, you will be more challenged to extend your compassion and love to the dirty alcoholic. This will be your test. Do not lose sight of unconditional love. Unconditional is the key word here. Suffering is its opposite. When you end the judgement of circumstances and others, you go into awakening and suffering ends. They all become the catalyst for positive change and opportunities for expansion.

Now let us address acceptance in more detail. Acceptance is knowing that all things, people, and situations are purposeful. Source doesn't make mistakes. It is experiencing and through that expands. So often I hear 'spiritual' people state that they wish others would wake up. They want others to stop suffering and to know their power. This is not acceptance. What would this journey be if they did not experience the suffering and pain you want to eliminate? There would be no lesson, no evolution, no expansion of the One. Wanting someone to change because you want the 'best' for them is stating 'You aren't OK' which is judgement. No one can know what is 'best' for anyone. Wanting the consequences from their choices to end is not accepting their free will. It is like wanting the baby to run before walking or to never experience the bruises from falling as they learn. What is the purpose of it all if not to know pain and contrast?

Christ could have changed his final chapter here, or avoided it. The man could walk on water and move mountains. Certainly, he could have opened the earth and had it swallow up his captors. But he didn't. We never would have the lessons had he not allowed the tragedy to play out. Because of it, he demonstrated that one can love and forgive even in the ultimate worst circumstance. Should we have changed that so that HE could avoid pain? That neighbor you wish to be happy, is learning. Wanting them to make different choices is a demonstration that YOUR ego is still in action. The only one that should consider change is the person not accepting the 'others journey.' It holds value, mostly to you. Can you simply love, serve others according to their choices and accept?

FREQUENCIES MATTER

Everything exists at all times in endless creations. All creations are simply expressions of One shared source. Appearing individual is One thing in all space and all times, endless and expansive, always transforming. Every form of itself exists in all time and holds equal intelligence and creative expression. Therefore, if each expression is endlessly connected to everything, then so are you. It goes on and on, and then it goes on beyond that. You are the very power you access and if you let go of all other programmed beliefs of what you are or what 'anything' is, you can literally perform miracles. We are endless expressions in endless dimensions. You have access to this at all times. It does not excuse you from any roles you chose that must play out, but perhaps you will now embrace that those can have different endings. All things are possible.

Don't you love it when scientists are adamant about 'how things work' only to switch gears when a new discovery is made? Science is fickle and continually produces new theories and facts that override what they claimed to be ultimate truth. Science is limited because it is a product of human thinking, no matter how advanced their techniques and experiments. Thoughts manifest? That was ridiculous nonsense to science until experiments revealed that the thoughts of the scientists were indisputably affecting results. How is that possible? All things are possible because all things are aware and intelligent. Science is another conduit for humans to try to understand that which it cannot. It is ego placing logic on something that has none. The One is a field beyond human logic. It is unlimited, can and does perform illogical feats.

Its intelligence is all things. Even chaos is organized intelligence appearing as chaos. Nothing is truly chaos nor accidental. There are no coincidences – only perfect cause and effect that humans cannot explain. The connections are obvious when one removes limited thinking.

The expression of the One intelligent energy comes in endless forms and is presented through vibrations. A lower vibration is a slower one, heavy and dense. We are a lower vibration. Each material illusion has a signature vibration that distinguishes a rock from a human from a cloud. Frequencies, however, have more flexibility. A dense human that raises his or her frequency may transcend the lower vibrational form it inhabits by accessing expansive powers beyond the body.

Allow me to simplify this complex subject. I shall refer to human frequencies in this explanation. Imagine a lower frequency as representing fear, separation, and attachment to the material world. It is limiting and the source of conflict. It is the opposite of unconditional love and compassion. If our matrix consisted of mansions, lower frequencies would reside in the basement. In that basement it is dark, moldy and dirty. Those in the basement fear one another and scrap for whatever they can find. They do not know what is in front of them as their sight is limited by the darkness. They know nothing beyond the basement.

Those in a higher frequency are loving, giving, and know that there is nothing to fear. They reside in the penthouse with amazing views. All are welcome there and are greeted with endless abundance and gifts. However, one must be on a high frequency to reach the penthouse. It is found by stepping on the elevator and going up to that top floor. The elevator is powered by frequency. If one raises his/her frequency, the elevator doors open, and they step on. It will rise to the floor of that person's frequency and let them off. He/she will join others on that floor. Perhaps it is the second or third floor. The higher floors reveal brighter spaces, more gifts and less conflict. The penthouse is enlightenment. It is this simple. All are the dimensions that we live in according to our frequency. Dimensions are simply realities in alignment with our frequency. They are not separate 'places' but realities that exist in the same time and space as all other expressions of the creator.

My Father has many mansions. There are endless spaces within the One energy that each of us can explore. This is why 'law of attraction' is not quite what has been presented. We will cover that subject next. A frequency is a chosen state of being through our beliefs and actions. The more loving, giving, compassionate, non-judgmental, fearless response, the higher the result. You are simply connecting to that which you choose that is 'like.' It cannot be any other way. Your vibration keeps you in your dense human form. Your frequency connects you to expansive powers, or not. It is a choice.

Singularity is the ultimate OVERALL goal. It is when all illusions played out, reach the One originating frequency and converge. That originating form is the highest frequency, unimaginable to humans. What comes after that? There is no 'after' in eternity. All exists and is interchangeable.

So why aren't we all choosing the penthouse? The lower frequencies believe in density as the 'all encompassing' reality. The ego is not interested in what it cannot see and touch. It seeks immediate material gratification. It understands its power not on the level of Oneness, but as a use for self-service. It battles for control and goods. It places 'self' first. This is the lowest frequency because anything below it self-destructs and exists in another dimension one might refer to as hell. Hell too, is a choice created through actions – cause and effect.

The ego uses this dense state of being to control others for its own agenda and therefore has had a great influence on our species.

137

After all, the game requires that we all start with a clean slate of ignorance. We do not know our origins or true powers and are susceptible to outside influences which make sense in a material world. Pain is real in our matrix game, and humans avoid it. Therefore, the majority continue to function as bodies in a material world, consumed with its battles and seeking solutions ongoing.

Frequencies are a choice. It is what tunes your radio station into rock and roll or classical music. What you tune into, you experience along with others in that same frequency. Therefore, all dense beings walk around as humans, but your frequency will determine your experience. We literally can shift into a different dimension within the human adventure. Dimensions are not necessarily other 'places' but other realities. Those dimensions form our experience which CAN manifest 'places.' Frequencies are experiences and vibrations are illusion manifestations. The dense low human body vibration has limitations as to what it can withstand, but it is possible to live in a higher frequency, thus dimension, within it. In that case, the higher frequency shifts into a the more expansive energy field. It opens the doors to the quantum consciousness where you access knowledge and abilities that lower frequencies cannot. This is how one person may see the world as a horrific place and another will live in bliss. Your intuition may heighten, and you could even experience time shifts and mystical events such as interacting with other beings.

The game, however, is simple. It is to raise our frequency back to that which is our source. Ah but here is the catch. We never lost that source and that frequency we seek is always within us. We always have access to it despite our vibrational limitations. It is what we refer to as the 'higher self.'

WHAT IS THE HIGHER SELF?

In typical human fashion, we believe that the higher self is some separate part of us 'out there somewhere' that we access on occasion. Most think of it as the pure, all knowing and powerful form of us that watches over our earthly persona. We think of it as a separate 'me' that operates as a guide and source of wisdom. If we are lucky or find some magical method to access it, we are privy to assistance and powers to guide us here on earth. That is not actually correct.

Simply stated, we are the higher self. It is you, right here, right now. You extend to the quantum, unending powerful field because there is no end to your energetic existence. Therefore, you are here, and there, and everywhere. You have access to all, right now as a human and the pure form of you that 'extends' outside of your body allows you pure decision-making resources that are unfettered by human intervention and thinking. It is the 'non-thinking' energy field of you that you can trust because it has no agenda. It is the essence of pure source that has a special interest in 'your' role here, making it the higher 'self' and not just the One source. While all in the same, each energy field plays out various roles. Your higher self is YOU in that safe zone guiding you at all times as One energy field. It cannot be anything else. You access it by 'tuning in' to it through a higher frequency. Meditation is a powerful method.

Why don't we simply use that resource all of the time? It is because the dense energy form of you, known as ego, still likes to control and boss you around. It will tell you that whatever messages you receive about being limitless and perfect are ridiculous nonsense that you are fabricating. After all, what are you going to trust, the body with a working brain or some unseen force that doesn't seem to take very good care of you most of the time? The ego wants proof of everything. Where is the higher self? If you can't prove its' existence, then why would you rely on it? Humans can't even tell when it's in action much less know how to use it.

The higher self is actually more 'you' than that person you see in the mirror. I speak of the intelligent energy that flows through all of us that chose these forms. It is the field with no material expression that creates and animates the material expression, bound with it for a brief period to play out roles. It is your conscious self. It is the driving force that flows with your adventure and allows the dense part of your persona to make mistakes, choose fear and play out scenarios. The more you recognize it, the more you awaken because it does not make decisions based on a material world. It is the purest energy form of you, animating your body at this moment with a conscious connection to all knowledge and power.

We live in a purposeful illusion that makes up the 'human game.' The Higher Self orchestrated it and is everything which we might refer to as the 'consciousness of God.' Everything comes from that consciousness, including unconsciousness. The higher self is your limitless extension. Know this and nothing else will be a problem for you.

The ultimate knowledge is that everything is an extension of one thing. Have you ever seen videos of UFO's that appear as one light, then split off into dozens, then converge again into one? That is how all 'things' function. We are always connected to the seen, and unseen worlds, separating and re-converging. Your higher self

140

is also a split of the higher power, connected at all times. Therefore, you are the One all-powerful field that knows all in all time and space. We are simply splitting off and re-converging as we explore and expand.

THE TIPPING POINT

I believe that quantum experiments simply reinforce what enlightened beings have always known. Everything is one thing 'happening.' All individual expressions are part of One power and One thing that appears in separate expressions in order to know separation. Separation is only one adventure. Cause and effect is constant as is expansion, and nothing escapes the influence of any other expression. You may place a dropper of red dye in the ocean believing that you don't make a difference, but that couldn't be further from the truth. Place enough droppers of red dye into those clear waters and things will eventually visibly change. They were already changing but we do not see it until the water looks a bit pink. Hmmm, something is not right here, and we continue to put red droppers of dye into the once clear blue water. Once it turns red, we have reached our tipping point when it is often too late to unwind the damage and thus, we suffer the extreme consequences. This is cause and effect that teaches us that there can be unpleasant repercussions to our choices. Humans need that visual or physical 'in your face' effect before we take action which is motivated by our ego's needs. When things are not to our satisfaction, we demand change. We don't like red water. We want clear blue water again even though we were responsible for the current conditions.

We have reached a tipping point and that is OK. Whatever it takes to evolve this planet is necessary and if 'in your face' pushes us to action, then we learn. We have not been concerned with consequences because responsibility often takes effort and the ego doesn't like to be inconvenienced. Its belief in endings means that it won't have to deal with the damage it causes today. Tomorrow's destruction as a result of its actions is something others will have to deal with. Humans ignore their actions and don't see themselves as the critically important contributors to all things. What is that one dropper of red water? It contributed to the final effect. Because we do not usually see the physical repercussions of our actions, we ignore what is going on in others realities. That plastic bottle you toss would mean more if it was all floating in your living room. Nothing is hidden from the quantum field. That includes that negative thought you have. It is forever and that choice you are making, positive or negative, within it reverberates throughout the universe. That thought is like the dropper in the ocean. It counts. Everything counts.

Having this kind of responsibility can be pretty scary when you realize you have such a powerful effect. This is not something you have some of the time. It is what you possess all of the time. We haven't taken it seriously enough. As I tell my YouTube viewers, you may think that it is just one plastic cup that you threw away, but when each ONE person with ONE cup is several billion, we now have an island of plastic cups the size of a small country floating in the ocean. If you were the fish swimming in that horror, your world would look very different. Yet we ARE that fish and we will know that pain when we reconnect to consciousness. We truly discount our importance and our choices.

What is a tipping point? Wherever and whenever there is a consistent imbalance, there is a push toward a result whether favored or not. It is when one 'side' dominates whether it be good, bad, light or darkness and through cause, an extreme effect occurs. Illness is a prime example. While the body is perfectly capable of defending itself against external and internal invaders, illness occurs when that defense team is imbalanced and the consistent push toward one side, takes over. It is no longer working as a community but as enemies in conflict, just as humans do. What was once living in harmony now battles for dominance and survival. Thus, a cold, flu, or a virus claims victory. This is a reflection of YOUR energy field because that internal community is connected to your thoughts and actions, and the frequency you choose.

But let us not judge each tipping point as 'bad.' They have often occurred due to the intolerance of injustice and abuse. Our challenge as humans has been to 'tip' in the favor of that which is highest and best for the collective and not small, self-serving groups. Somehow, we seem to miss that important step and slide back into 'me' and decide that what 'I' want is best for everyone. Tipping points prompt action because they usually cause great discomfort for egos. Unfortunately, most actions to 'fix' the problems do not create new and healthy foundations, but simply patch them. Our foundations are crumbling. This is a positive tipping point that will force us to make bigger choices. With our push toward a higher frequency, I feel that those choices will serve others and not simply look to patch a material world that no longer works for the betterment of any of its inhabitants.

Our planet has been in great turmoil since humans appeared. The cycle of tipping points has been a part of our existence, correcting itself when necessary but only when pushed to great imbalance that causes discomfort. We are now at a massive, critical tipping point that could very well end our existence here altogether if we choose that direction. Is that a bad thing? The question is 'should destruction and violence come to an end?' If your answer is 'yes,' then the end of the human species would not be bad. Is that necessary? Of course not. So far, however, we have not chosen those higher options. We continue to operate as individuals when community and cooperation as a unified collective could easily bring us back into balance. Working as a community and service to others would easily end destruction and violence without blasting ourselves into oblivion. It certainly would be a more pleasant way to shift our reality.

Every illness, war, and conflict on our planet is a tipping point of the collective actions. Nothing stands alone. These events are not a result of one cause or argument. They are an accumulation of beliefs, thoughts, emotions and eventually actions over a period of time. No pandemic, financial collapse, or destruction of any kind 'just happened.' They are a long, accumulation of choices and actions, all of which were never stable in the first place. I liken it to those who appear to spontaneously awaken. Nothing is spontaneous. Spontaneous awakening, although we believe happens in a moment, always followed a series of events. Eckhart Tolle is a great example. His desire to end his life resulted in a spontaneous awakening. However, he spent a lifetime in unhappiness. Even as a child, he had thoughts of suicide. That is hardly spontaneous. It was the accumulation of a lifetime of pain and finally a tipping point, a choice to exit that lead to the release of the source of his pain – the ego. It was then that the light was able to fully shine. Without the story the ego claimed, there was nothing else to struggle with.

We love to blame those in power as the culprit, replacing them with new leaders who will 'fix everything,' only to find out that not much has changed. We see a pandemic spreading and seek to blame one source, ignoring the chain of events that brought us to that tipping point. We scratch and claw to 'maintain' our material existence which is acceptable within our society until we 'tip' and it becomes quite inconvenient for us. So, we scratch and claw for new resources to 'fix' our problems at the cost of others' or our planet's wellbeing. Repercussions from our actions are always in play. Every action, every thought contributes to a healthy balance or a tipping point, one way or the other. We CAN tip to peace and release of the ego, the great awakening, and redemption. It will take work, but it is not too late.

The tipping point is always a reflection of the primary focus of our beliefs and actions. We 'tip' toward that which we 'are.' We think of tipping points as being either positive or negative, but both ultimately lead to one conclusion and that is the universal scream, 'Here is what you think. You can change it!'

Our human dilemma is to know that even if 'that world out there' is not panning out as desired, we still control our own 'inner world.' The world 'out there' is not separate from you and even if YOU did your very best, it is not a guarantee of a higher outcome for the planet as a whole. Herein is the confusion of the human brain which wants ME to control THAT as a whole. Yes, we are a whole energy field, but you, within the collective, choose your own experience, while the collective has its own tipping point. Everyone contributes toward it and part of the agreement you made was to influence that outcome. Nothing gets you out of this responsibility. Whether you make higher or lower choices is up to you regardless of your plan before you came here. Everything is in a state of change and flexible. Free will offers the choice of any outcome no matter how dire the circumstance. Complacency is an illusion and is just as much a contributing factor as action. It is time for action.

I am sorry to inform you my friend, that ANYONE not making higher decisions is responsible for our planetary woes. Blaming others fools no one. In fact, judgement and criticism of those 'problem people' is not only equally detrimental but is the source of conflict. The universe does not hear arguments, it simply reacts to frequencies as requests and delivers them like a cosmic Amazon. Judgement and blame are equally destructive as the actions of the wrongdoers being blamed.

The universe does not judge right nor wrong and even though it is the supreme intelligence of all things, it does not 'think.' It KNOWS and has total acceptance. It created the right and wrong as part of the options of the players in our games. How can that be wrong? It is like saying that the Joker should not be a part of

146

the Batman series. Without Jokers, there would be no reason to have a Batman. This is the 'purpose' that we seek to play out. The Source and its endless options present unending stories. From the stories we tell ourselves, we then act upon them and all actions produce a reaction. Sometimes results are immediate, sometimes it takes a little longer, but it always delivers. Time matters not in the metaverse. Each thought is heard without delay and is in play.

When you judge another, you live in the world of victimization and separation. Each player is pointing the finger at the other. "You are wrong and the problem to my woes (or the world or society, or . . .)." The perpetrators of destruction feel equally as strong about their justifications as you do. Who is right? Everyone is right because 'right' is whatever you decide for YOU and the collective shares that contribution. You are gifted with the ability to reside in your own reality while existing in the shared one that is this matrix that we play in. Who else is within that frequency with you? Either a community of positive change makers, or others that blame, judge, and look after their own best interests and opinions. Have you heard the phrase 'like attracts like?' There you go. Expect nothing else. When you judge you are judged. When you love, you are loved. Compassion given will be received when YOU need it most whether you or anyone believes you deserve it or not. The field of all intelligence operates on equality at all times. There is no 'thought' behind this.

There are many who believe that they are not contributing to the collective tipping point because they choose not to participate. However, taking no action is also a contributor to the collective. It is 'service to self' because that decision is due to one desiring to protect their own interests by retreating from any responsibility. It is easier for 'me' to retreat than to make an effort. Efforts can result in pain and challenges, so the 'me' that does nothing is actually ego protecting itself. This is fear.

It is understandable that some desire to do nothing. Perhaps you have tried to make a positive impact and become frustrated or disheartened when you see that nothing has really changed at all. Even when the world seems to be crashing down around you when you are making all of the 'right' choices, I assure you that you are making a difference. Never underestimate your power and importance. Your choices, both big and small, contribute toward the collective outcomes in amazing and powerful positive ways. Like the plastic cup that contributes to the billions of others, when you decide that you will not contribute to it, your impact reverberates. Others will follow suit. Never forget that your positive choices affect YOUR personal tipping points and take YOU to amazing spaces of expansion and love. You receive what you give, even if the material world does not seem to reflect it. So, if the tipping point is total planetary destruction, your tipping point can still be awakening and peace. You can move on to a different collective knowing that you did your best. Your personal and the collective's reality do not have to be the same just as your neighbor's will be different. Realities are limitless. You get to choose yours.

Our existing way of life is not sustainable. We know this but ego will continue to fight for what it knows. How do we change this dangerous cycle of destruction? We must focus on solutions. Solutions offer expansion and when in expansion mode, the quantum field sends insights, ideas, and inspiration. If we do not find new ways and solutions to our current way of life, eventual disaster is in store. Good news. Tipping points CAN be reversed in any direction.

Let us take a look at what appears to be 'beyond your control' versus actions that have obvious and predictable results. For example, are you really responsible for those abusive parents, the car accident, being born into poverty and other seemingly random situations? Yes. You are a contributor by choice because nothing stands alone. All of us are the One experiencing everything. Therefore, we are ALL choosing, creating, and expanding. We contribute toward it all with those choices and actions. This is a movement of energy that culminates in a series of events. Some is prior to our arrival here. No one choice stands alone even though it may appear that things 'just happen.' When examined further there are direct causes of all results whether subtle over a long period of time, or obvious.

Nothing 'happens to you' without your participation. That is impossible. You are part of that force that is exploring every possible form of itself. You have been creating and choosing since eternity and that future of yours is a moving target based on every decision you make NOW. That is why predictions are actually warnings more than events set in stone. They are insights into a future based on current choices (thoughts, beliefs, actions). Isn't it wonderful to know that you can change any outcome? Even actions that are taking you to what might be disaster can be remedied. There are always lessons to learn from them, but final outcomes are interchangeable and endless. Then there were decisions you made before you came into your human role that are meant to play out. Don't overthink this. Just know that you are always in control and the universe is playing out according to YOUR choices, always. You only need to choose the highest and best response at every moment. This requires awakening, also known as consciousness.

The tipping point is a result of choices along unlimited time lines before, during and beyond our human existence. They are nexus points that converge and take us down totally different pathways as a result of those choices. These can come in the form of an epiphany or something as obvious as a building collapsing that was built on sand.

Very often we work toward a tipping point with no noticeable success. Then, one day, something unexpected shifts us into a major change. The gossip at work eventually gets us fired when the new boss arrives. The heart attack occurs after years of physical neglect. Of course, it happens equally as often for positive outcomes. That nexus point is the convergence of focus. The months of eating healthy and exercising took us to that moment when we tipped into completing a marathon. And so, we must be patient as each grain of sand is added to the scale along with a few boulders along the way. It is like being that player on the field wherein the entire game rests on that one goal kick. That kicker is truly the final grain of sand to the tipping point, but we know that the game actually rested on the performance of all of the players up until that moment, starting with that first kickoff. It all counts.

THIS IS YOUR SPIRITUAL BUTT KICK

Why a 'butt kick?' Because you are powerful beyond your imagination. Because we know through the very small discoveries in quantum physics and other demonstrations that we do hold that power. Because it's our duty to evolve and to raise our and the planet's frequency that will catapult us into pure glory humans have never known. Because this is the game you signed up for. BECAUSE YOU ARE POWERFUL AND YOU ARE READY!

Your tattered clothes are lined with jewels. Reach into your pockets. The treasures of the universe reside there. You have no limits. You hold magic and the fear that has held you back has been your gift to know this. Yet we still choose to cling to ignorance because it is familiar. I suspect that if you are reading or listening to this, you are past begging your angels to save you, praying without results, learning law of attraction techniques to get 'stuff', and finding that nothing has changed for you. You are not alone. Nothing that you achieve is a result of a 'technique.' Techniques only work through belief. It is simply what I call the 'knowing' of 'all that is' of which you never disconnected from. I believe that the world is waking up in a BIG way and that awakening is coming in like a lion, and WILL go out like a lamb and remain in that state until our next chapter. When this happens is up to us. Anything is possible.

So, what, exactly is a spiritual butt kick? It's when we take a good look at ourselves, our beliefs, our actions and thoughts, and take responsibility for all of it. After all, you are the one that controls those thoughts and actions despite any challenges you have experienced throughout this human journey. The 'kick' is that nudge that most of us need to actually get out onto the playing field and to realize that if we don't do our best, our team cannot win.

Allow me to introduce your 'spiritual butt kick' that can get you in the game and rushing down the field for a touchdown. The team and the crowd will cheer and, of course, then we go back and do it all over again. There is good news. The championship match can be won, and you can retire your uniform and move onto a new game, softer, with less bruises. You may get bored with gardening perfect flowers and vegetables that never fail, perfect weather, and perfect relationships. You might just find yourself signing up for a comeback performance, a new challenge, maybe even to master fear.

We each have a mission. This is a critical period in our illusion of earth time. You are one of the few light beings that chose to participate in the transformation of human history. No matter how disempowered you may feel, your presence here alone is proof that you are a chosen energy field with great purpose. Transitioning into unconsciousness is a massive undertaking. There is no guarantee that you will achieve consciousness during your trip here. However, you will return to that state when you leave density. Remember, this is a matrix; a hologram, and not the true essence of you. You, along with many other forces in the universe planned and chose this human identity that you are living out.

Like you, I too have a mission. I wasn't always a spiritual butt kicker. I was actually a shy kid and if you looked at me, I might hide. I never liked Santa Claus and always cried when my Aunt and Uncle placed me on that old man's lap for a picture. The idea of telling some stranger what I wanted for Christmas made no sense and I endured the experience for the sake of my Aunt and Uncle who did not have kids at the time. In fact, I found a lot of human practices uncomfortable. I very much preferred playing alone in my bedroom and the world did not make a lot of sense. I didn't like attention and frankly, still don't. But when we grow up and become big boys and girls, we must often do things we don't like in order to fulfill our purpose and achieve our goals. Sometimes the thing you are best at may not be the thing you want to do. You get to decide how you use your gifts. When you place service to others first, despite how uncomfortable it may be, it is always a higher more purposeful choice. It challenges you and through challenges we expand. Expansion is a high frequency. Expand.

Many here find life uncomfortable most of the time. Life takes you exactly where you need to be and where you asked to be. Yes, YOU ASKED to be. Remember that part about taking responsibility? Let's get to the nitty gritty. YOU planned this journey, YOU AGREED to specific challenges, YOU aligned circumstances in order to create tests for yourself, and YOU CHOSE to come to Earth to master all of them. If you are whining about it then you are choosing disempowerment and unfortunately, that is what the majority of humans choose. We see all of it as a grueling, often useless journey with some pleasures and mostly pain.

So, I want to ask you a critical question. WHO or WHAT do you think is in charge of all of this? If not you, then who - God, or whatever ultimate source that you believe in? If so, then my next question is 'Is this ultimate source good or bad?' Did you answer 'good?' If so, then what do you think the purpose of a planet of pain would offer? Do you think this 'good' ultimate source created it all to inflict torture on its inhabitants? Do you think that this Source of all is finding enjoyment in seeing such struggle? Is this a chaotic situation or is there some kind of order in it all? Is there another Source that inflicts evil? If so, who or what created it? If there is one creator, then that One MUST have created everything. Right?

Let's recap what we have covered so far. There is nothing separate. That Source is everything, including you. There is no torture or unplanned activity that goes without your approval and willing participation because YOU are IT. IT is everything. He, She, God, Source, One . . . we are all IT. And IT is experiencing every facet of itself through us, the trees, clouds, planets, and every other life form both seen and unseen that humans cannot begin to comprehend. This isn't my opinion but is in alignment with quantum physics. We are entangled. We are all that is seen and unseen. Nothing is separate. That means that we are One Big happy energy experiencing the contrast that allows us to KNOW that the garden in any condition is perfect and that all weather is amazing. It is experiencing loss because IT in its perfect expression, its highest frequency, never experiences loss. It wants to know loss to know eternity. This is what planet Earth supplies, and YOU chose to experience this amazing, insane, beautiful, perfect and painful adventure. You are a collector of data and information through experiences. When you come to terms with this, you will be empowered in ways you never thought possible.

Are you ready to empower yourself? If so, then get ready to be amazed because YOU as the ONE energy, have no limits. Yes, you chose to be a human in a specific role at this Earth time which means that self-imposed planetary and human limits are in place. These too, however, can be broken. For instance, Christ walked on water and Moses parted it. There are no limits except those that you believe. Believe and receive is real. Your belief creates your reality and mine creates mine. No two realities or experiences are alike. As humans, we expect that there is One reality and One correct response that all must adhere to. This egotistical thinking and separatism are at the root of all conflict. It pits the entire team against one another, chaotically running around the playing field beating one another up, tripping and kicking every player it comes in contact with. This is coming to an end.

154

Do you know what you are? Do you know why all of 'THIS' is so uncomfortable? It's because none of it is natural for us and deep down, we know that it seems 'wrong.' Yet we did choose it and that is the most confusing part. How can we witness the suffering and torture and 'choose' that? Each person is responsible for his or her actions, so of course we are choosing. You can say that you did not choose an abusive upbringing, but your parents chose to treat you a certain way. That means that you participated in the scenario because you DID make the decision to be a part of that experience. YOU CHOSE them, THEY CHOSE you and all of you choose your responses. Chances are that they came from abuse too. Their parents had the choice to inflict pain or to love. With those choices, your parents could follow suit or break the pattern. You now have the torch and get to decide what YOU will do with all of this. Blame and anger are simply reinforcing their lower frequency choices, yet we usually don't see it that way. We like to justify our own negative thoughts and actions. Then nothing changes and we say that the 'world is bad' yet we are the direct cause of it all. We must break the chain of programming if we want to effect great change.

You probably guessed by the book title that this wasn't going to be a 'feel good, fuzzy, fluffy' kind of read. You won't find any statements that reassure you that it is okay to hate your parents or any persons whom have harmed you. Nor will you find sympathy for your woes. It is not because I don't have compassion for you, because I do. The reason is that we have moved past years of psychoanalysis for something we believe should never have happened and have now progressed to knowing that everything is purposeful, perfect and chosen by you. No one is a victim and that is one of the most difficult truths to recognize.

Awakening has opened the door to truths that we cannot deny. The blinders are off, and we now have information that no matter how 'wrong' we are told we are, we know in our hearts that there is so much more to our existence. With proof revealed by quantum mechanics, we know that we are not only entangled with all that occurs around and to us, but that we direct those situations. Entanglement pulls the sole responsibility off of us and places us as willing participants with the actions of others. Nothing works quite like when we recognize that we are a community that is much more powerful working in alignment with service to others. It is time to recognize the purpose of it all, that you are simply all that you seek to access, are the awareness of all that 'happens' and the cause. That is that. When you comprehend this, you can change everything. You can stop seeing everything as an accident or punishment, stop blaming others, and start doing your part. Knowing that it is all intentional, only then will the collective receive the message of change and rise above it all. Of course, that is unless you prefer to continue suffering and perpetuating the negative patterns that will be the final destruction of the planet. You get to choose.

In conclusion, you are Source. You are eternal, all powerful, and perfect. Know this without thoughts or explanations. Is it time to plan out your journey? Is there something you have held back on? Perhaps there are things you want to do, to accomplish in your lifetime but you lacked faith in yourself. Have you listened to the world and its limitations for so long that you believe them? Do you place the opinions of others before your own? When you choose passion, giving, compassion and faith, you accelerate expansion. Expansion is a space where solutions, inspiration, opportunities and answers lie. Ask your guides to show you the way, and do the work.

LET GO AND LET GOD

You may have heard the term, "Let Go and Let God." Most have, but what does it mean? Simply stated, it is the most effective, fastest, direct way to ultimate creativity, inspiration and positive, desired, manifestation. It takes one into community and harmony which is health, wealth, and happiness. It is also the biggest challenge for humans because we are ruled by the ego that wants full control the way it wants and when it wants it. Therefore, 'letting go' of anything is a dilemma despite the promise of peace and prosperity. The ego believes that it knows best and cannot fathom relinquishing oversight of anything. After all, the ego believes that it is separate from everything else, therefore, who or what could possibly make better decisions for it?

Why is letting go required to go into that powerful space of manifesting miracles? What does that do for us that we can't do for ourselves? Simply put, choices made by the ego come from a self-serving space that perpetuates separation and disharmony within the energetic communities of all things. When we expand into the higher mind, we access the massive and endless probabilities that serve all. We know that what we give, we receive. Therefore, service to others is service to self in the most expansive form. This is the higher self we speak of which is the energetic field of YOU, without the control of density-based unconsciousness. The higher self is what we all have access to as humans. In fact, it is what we ARE. It is the purest form of our energy field that can do anything. It is not of this material world yet creates and experiences it.

Energy is Source and exists in everything. This is the true God. Letting go is the relinquishing of the dense, controlling ego

157

to the higher, unlimited power of the One that is always working in your favor. It must, because it has no agenda nor judgement. It is simply Source operating on expansion in its highest frequency. That frequency is love.

Stepping aside is not an easy task. Humans believe in what they 'see' and can touch. They battle to acquire and maintain this material world and its circumstances. It is a world that although is ever changing, humans cling to for both our short-term survival and pleasure. The goal is to exist as long as possible despite the constant struggle that humans bring upon themselves. How amazing that humans choose to create, participate in and extend pain and volatility. This certainly is a planet inhabited by an insane species.

Let us address the subject of miracles. Miracles can happen in two major ways. First, they occur when one lets go because the controlling thinking mind no longer interferes with its unlimited capabilities. The second is when the receiver 'believes' in the unknown power and that 'it' can do something that he or she cannot. Both are forms of release of the ego's grip on control. This is why an atheist or 'sinner' as we label others, can receive a miracle while someone loyal to religion may not. It is simply the release of the ego to that power. Often times, those with preconceived ideas of who is deserving or how miracles happen are the most closed to receiving it. The 'letting go' is the release of these beliefs or thoughts which is why those without structured beliefs may be the most receptive. Because the miracle 'space' does not judge but simply acts on directives, this opens the way for any human to receive a miracle or any other manifestation. You see, it's an equal playing field not reserved for 'good' people or 'religious' ones. The clear message 'yes, this is possible,' is all that is needed. Faith is a powerful directive and the ultimate letting go that allows amazing probabilities to materialize.

Now let us talk about the other way humans 'let go.' This is done through what we know as the 'dark night of the soul.' It is that place we visit when the ego is exhausted, nothing it tries is working, it moves beyond being desperate, and relinquishes all power. It is a place of no hope and bottomless darkness. This is the most undesirable pathway to a miracle, because it is the most painful. It can also be the most effective because it is extreme and a total release of the ego control and misdirection. At this point, there is nothing more to cling to. When one comes to this conclusion, all barriers are removed, and a pure and unfettered pathway opens up. Miracles happen. FINALLY! The highest, purest, most loving power is now in control through invitation. There is silence, with no more voices of 'how things are' that limit the higher self from taking charge. Amazing manifestations then appear! Awakening happens.

How simple this seems, yet so amazingly difficult at the same time. All of it is thanks to the programmed ego that stands in the way of its own desires. No one need suffer on such a deep, painful level in order to let go. In fact, you can let go right now. How? You no longer need to believe the stories it tells nor or try to stop them. When you try to stop thinking, you struggle. You battle with yourself and inner turmoil accelerates. Instead, observe thoughts like clouds and smile. "There it goes again," might be a thought with no reaction to it, and the mind chatter will eventually dissolve. When this occurs, a feeling of lightness floods in. The energy space is cleared of the limitations and problems. There is nothing but peace with no agenda, no requirements and nothing is 'needed' to be happy. Happiness becomes a state of being and everything else is a bonus. Simply let go.

WHAT IS AWAKENING?

When we fail to acquire the material world to our satisfaction or have successfully acquired it only to find that it did not produce that elusive happiness we expected, we suffer. That definition of happiness, of course, is according to our personal requirements despite what happens in the world around us. The desire to feel good is constant and our ego seeks it in every way possible on its terms. Those terms are always changing because nothing is ever enough for the ego to be satisfied. When it experiences happiness, it always wants more. Getting more is its job.

The ego believes that it is in control by manipulating the outside world. This results in the most dense, low frequency state of being. Why is it the lowest frequency? It is concerned with the 'self' above all and only cares about others if 'they' supply its needs. This desire for power and control over its circumstances and others is the cause of wars, hoarding, anger, arguments and hatred. It must gain as much as possible in the case that someone else may obtain it first. Then what? More chaos, more conflict, more problems. It cares about nothing else beyond what it sees and feels. Multiply the planet's population with controlling egos and nothing but conflict exists. Any joy it experiences is temporary and based on alliances with others that serve mutual egos' desires. These egos, however, will turn on one another when not in alignment with the individual's needs. There is no trust in the circle of egos.

Then the inevitable happens. The ego causes more pain than happiness when its mission fails. As it becomes more unhappy, frustration, doubts, maybe even anger grow, setting its host (you) up for a major crash. It may appear as chronic depression, mood swings, or physical illness. These lower frequencies manifest in endless destructive ways because nothing works in harmony on this level. The ego then reaches back out to the material world for a 'fix' through medications, excessive drug or alcohol use, more control over others, overeating and self-hatred. There are plenty of other egos ready to reinforce these choices and offer escapes. It then may blame those sources and strike out in anger and blame. Anger and blame are favorite choices. Sometimes it reaches out for awakening. Yes! Awakening! THAT will give it happiness! Or so it thinks. It cannot understand nor know that awakening is only achieved through the ego's death.

Even in our most desperate moments, the ego seeks ways to get out of its situation through the outside world. This is often the catalyst for awakening but can also lead to unspeakable, desperate, and self-destructive acts. Whether it seeks awakening or crime, its mission is to eliminate anything unpleasant according to its definition and on its terms. The ego is all about me and what I have or what I get. It values nothing but satisfaction gained through fulfilling its desires and avoids everything else. The need to acquire what makes it happy is never ending which means that humans will always suffer when it is in charge. The 'stuff' goes away, the material joy wears off, the job or relationship ends, or it runs out of things that please it. The message is clear. Wake up! There is another way that is even more powerful, more joyful, more amazing but, the ego is lazy and avoids the stairway to heaven because it just does not want to have to climb those stairs! That is work! We want the elevator or a private jet to take us there, the lottery ticket, the hot guy or gal to make us feel desirable, or the physical 'high.' Yet, those unpleasant life situations, keep showing up with the reminder to 'wake up! This is why you are here!' We battle the message and we suffer, and suffer, and suffer. And we pass on our program of suffering to others.

So, what happens when life isn't working for us; when that ego no longer delivers and instead leads us to despair? What happens when the 'stuff' no longer satisfies us, and we find ourselves worse off for it all? It is only when all appears to be lost and the ego is no longer our trusted friend that we are in the wonderful position to 'let go.' Letting go means releasing all control, not having the answers and not trying to find them. It is the release of the material world that is not giving us all that we had hoped for and the release of needs, requirements and ambition. This can be the unexpected blessing no one deliberately chooses to experience. It can be painful. Hitting rock bottom is the most profound experience and gateway to spiritual freedom. But you do not have to go there to awaken.

While great suffering can lead to awakening, this passage into hell does not always result in finding paradise. The 'dark night of the soul' has no such guarantee. The ego may hold fast and whisper that someone or something in the material world will save it. The sufferer then makes desperate attempts to solve its problems as she or he usually does, by finding what it needs to 'make things right.' This causes even more suffering and the cycle of pain continues. Or in some instances, the experiencer simply slides into the depths of despair with no hope of recovery. Many have spent lifetimes in this state of density. It is a space so dark that they find it impossible to see any light of which to find their way out.

There are always opportunities to evolve whether in this lifetime or another. It is the mission of every illusion. Evolution does not necessarily mean achieving an enlightened state, but can simply be the exploration of all things. It all contributes to the constant growth of the Source knowledge. More information is supplied through trials and tribulations just as much as triumphs. Just being here is a big step toward that contribution. Pain and controversy are not easy paths to endure.

One can end the conversation with the ego that continually produces havoc. The screams for control become whispers and eventually the whispers cease. Awakening finds an opening when the ego stops talking and the sufferer realizes that "I am still here." There is then a realization that everything needed 'already is' and always has been. It was never lost. Awakening is the moment when one reaches into the tattered robe pockets and finds that they are full of jewels. Awakening is the recognition that everything 'out there' is not who we are but that which we create. It is then that empowerment beyond human comprehension takes charge and miracles are every day events. The release of material desires may sound difficult, but it is required to end struggle. The good news is that it is then that material abundance opens up to us with ease. The world then 'appears' different, because we choose to see it differently. It is not a space full of material goods and situations but one of beauty and opportunities. Gratitude for that which flows to us dominates, sending the message 'I have,' and so it is.

Awakening is a mystery. If one has never experienced such a state in their current human form, how can he or she know what they are looking for, or the secret to inviting it? Even those who claim to be in an awakened state cannot truly define 'what' it is or what transpired. It is like trying to understand what chocolate tastes like if you have never had any. For those who have, describing the taste cannot convey the experience. One must taste chocolate him or herself. Herein is the dilemma because coming from the ego's mind to find awakening is the opposite of what it is. It is not to be found. The pathway to awakening from a place of no understanding is the ultimate challenge. There is no one formula to awakening. It is your unique journey and like any destination, not all arrive. It is discovering the clearing after wandering in the deep, dark woods.

Buddha spent years dedicated to understanding and overcoming human suffering before transitioning into enlightenment. He tried every known method to achieve it until finally 'going into nothingness' took him there. A rest under the Bodhi tree lead him to transformation. A great many transition into this state not by seeking it so much as letting go of worldly demands, not understanding what happened to them. I experienced such a state of being. The interesting part of awakening with no knowledge of what it is, nor intentionally seeking it is that you don't need to know or understand it. Those in an awakened state stop asking questions. Only the ego desires to label and understand that which is not understandable. All is in order and that which is unknown is not a mystery to solve. It is the ultimate state of peace, a frequency of being. I call it 'the knowing.' The knowing is not needing to know and totally accepting all.

So, you see that seeking awakening is fueled by the ego's desire to 'get' something which, ironically, can never be found in that state of being. The message that is sent by this desire is 'I'm not OK' or 'Perfection is outside of me.' And, so it is. When the ego gives up, awakening finds an opening. The barriers are removed. However, seeking specific teachings and practices, spending years or maybe a lifetime in search cannot be a mistake. There is great satisfaction and enjoyment in exploring ascension. It is all part of the experience and process of simply knowing that we never had to find it. It was always just 'who' and 'what' we are. The rest is adventure.

Awakening is the center balance point of a teeter totter. You might remember that long board we used to play on as kids. Each person sat on one end and would push off to lift up and then down again. If one were to get off of the teeter totter while the other was in the up position, they would come crashing down. When we live in density, we are always on one end or the other; up or down. Awakening is the center point, never going up nor down, but balancing the good and bad, naming neither. It does not experience the extremes of the emotional ego, but allows the role of the experiencer to know human feelings without the trauma and negative stories attached. Awakening is observation of the feelings and experiences, while remaining in a state of calm.

Why is awakening such an elusive state of being? It is because humans think of it as something 'out there' and as long as the 'stuff' is making us happy, there is no incentive to change that. If one is unhappy, it's time for a new job, a new car, a new relationship or a vacation. We think of awakening as having to give up the things that we enjoy the most. "Will I have to give up my expensive sports car or designer purses?" The answer is 'Of course not!' In fact, you will enjoy them even more and find satisfaction with the things you have. Because you no longer need them to be happy, you will share them and find more joy in simplicity. Awakening will enhance your joy within the material world, but not in the way you may think. It does not require anything because it is complete, but appreciates and is grateful for the material world.

So, let's talk about that 'incentive' to awaken. What drives us to want to awaken and what is awakening anyway? What is the purpose? If it is something so unknown to us, why do so many seek it? Why aren't we in that state of bliss in the first place? The truth is that most find no need for it nor have any desire to explore the spiritual realms because they are so entrenched in the material world that they cannot identify with anything else. It is only when life no longer serves us, and our back is up against the wall, that we seek every possible option. Let us be totally honest here. If you have the ideal relationship, ideal job, financial freedom, and health, what else is there? Life is bliss and perfect. Ah, but we know that never lasts for long. The thrill wears off, the job ends, the money comes and goes, our health is compromised, and we grow old. When the material world stops producing satisfaction, the ego wants to fix it. It is at this point that the ego looks for alternatives.

Perhaps happiness comes with awakening or so the ego believes. Yes, that's it! Awakening is the answer! That mystical place MUST be the solution, and so the ego's search begins for its new 'high.'

Seeking that which cannot be touched or perceived in the material world is like describing light to a blind man. The most baffling part is that so few seem to achieve it. Why? Who is allowed into this seemingly secret club? Is there a special passage way or technique? Are some predestined to gain entry? Are these members privileged or special? I am happy to share some important information with you. There is a formula to awakening. It is a simple one but the most difficult for humans who desire it most. Awakening comes through letting go of the importance of the physical world, its situations and conditions. This includes the beliefs and thoughts you may have always identified with. It is knowing that we are not 'this' nor 'that' but are all things and that this is an opportunity of massive proportions. It is letting go of judgment, anger and blame within this journey. It is letting go of the stories, about everything. It is 'no thought.' Awakening is the release of the human state of limitations.

YOU ARE ALREADY AWAKENED – YOU CAME HERE THAT WAY – IT IS WHAT YOU ARE – EVERYTHING ELSE IS ILLUSION

Everyone knows that children are pure. To see the world through a child's eyes is to see it without negative stories, programming, or limitations. It includes magic, fairies and unlimited dimensions. Children enter the world in the state of awakening. Childish fear is real because children are the essence of purity now infused with the density of a body that is exposed to a very uncomfortable, often unloving world. Threats and unpleasant experiences are new to the loving spirit force. These same pure spirits are then exposed to adults that they naturally trust who then pass on their own fears and limitations. The dark veils continue to pile on and obscure the light of the new adventurer.

Ironically, we are so concerned about child predators and similar threats, yet main society does far more damage to our newer explorers who are taught distortions. This is not always intentional because ignorance teaches ignorance. We believe that we 'protect' children by reinforcing fear and then send them out into a world that now appears to be filled with constant threats. We expose them to violent media and games, prejudices and gossip, separation, and rules. If they do not learn or behave in an acceptable manner, they are fed pharmaceuticals that will 'fix' the condition. The fairies then disappear, and the monsters begin to appear. The programming has been established and the once unlimited thinkers now function fully in the program of the limited matrix. We teach them that killing is a game and peace is sought through wars. Ego and its need for power, control, and to fulfill its endless greed now rules. They seek acceptance from others, winning, and no longer share that unconditional love that came so naturally.

You were no different. You came here in that state of awakening. We all arrive awakened until the material world becomes real and to speak of those fairies is discouraged because magic is dangerous to ruling egos. The ghosts and invisible friends can no longer be seen and retreat as the adults convince us that they are a part of our imagination. We learn limitations and suffering. The heavy burden of the world takes over and we forget what we are. Yes, you came here awakened and you still are. The rest is a story that you started to believe and probably still do. That is a choice. Those veils can be removed. They are illusions. You are complete and always will be.

HOW does one achieve that beautiful state of being wherein no situation is a problem, no person is an enemy (no matter how evil), and challenges have clear meaning? By releasing all that is human, all that is illusion, the stories that limit you, you will pass through the gateway to your perfection. When illusion is released all that is left is love. It was always there, it always is, always will be. When there are no more thoughts or stories, there is just one, beautiful energy field of expansion, exploring, experiencing. You just ARE. I am that, I am, and all is THAT and all is One. There are no questions in this space. No answers are needed.

Ah, but how to release everything? How is this formula to awakening implemented? The answer, once again, is simple. You are already that which you seek. The essence of you is the creator of you and animates that 'you' that you relate to. Observe the limiting stories and fears that the ego whispers. Battle nothing. Know its origins and stop seeing it as an enemy but as an ignorant protector operating from the lowest frequency. Watch thoughts float by like clouds. Do not analyze nor interact with them. The quiet mind holds power because nothing exists there except light. View your ego as an ancient protector within the material world that has served a positive purpose and, used wisely, still can. Despite its seeming individual power that holds its own dialogue, it is not a threat, nor does it control you. That is impossible since it is generated by you.

Although we master the human game by recognizing this pure power that we are, never forget that the veils and the illusions are not mistakes. They are created by you and in agreement with others who play in your game. Amazing experiences come from this adventure. Endless opportunities for greatness, acts of unselfishness and love are constantly presented. This is what it's all about! You desired to know this state and perhaps it is time to end the cycle of ignorance. This is the true challenge. Can we go from Oneness and perfection to total ignorance and density only to rediscover our perfection? What a great game. We cannot achieve this without the challenge of density.

Most humans believe that awakening is a rare occurrence reserved for few and to achieve it is a long, drawn out monumental task. We, in our density, consider awakened ones as separate and 'different' to the masses. We have rules about what an awakened person is and how they should act. We often think of 'spiritual' humans as speaking with a soft voice, always having a serene smile and holding the answers to the universe. They certainly would never swear, drink alcohol, or smoke. WRONG! Individual human expression means that the unkempt beggar on the street could be the angel in disguise. Your obnoxiously loud Aunt could be enlightened, and your spiritual teacher whom you believe has all of the answers may be unknowingly preaching fear. You see, to be human is to experience contrast for all participants. All of it. It's part of the package and no matter what awakened state you achieve here, as long as you reside in a body, you cannot escape its density. No one can truly know if another is awakened except through intentions. Yes, awakening will prompt a change in many behaviors such as eating habits and even the friends you choose to hang out with, but never forget that no matter what state of awakening you are in, you do not escape challenges. Never assume that the 'other' is somehow the problem, however, know that you do not have to choose to hang out with them. This is not judgement so much as a choice to keep a clear energy field.

No matter what frequency you live in, all other forms within our matrix are equal. No one has power over you, nor can you infringe on another's free will no matter how hard you try. All of us are equal in our abilities, our choices, and our importance. Never forget this.

Awakening is a choice. There is nothing to 'achieve.' Once you peel back the layers of 'you,' you will find nothing. No thoughts. No unruly emotions or judgement, no desires, no threats. You have everything and through this knowledge, you are able to give without fear of lack. You will know fear as the ego's whispers in a world it believes and learn to observe it, understand its source, and break through it. Fear is just an experience.

I am one of those personalities that would not last long in a monastery. I wasn't meant to. As soon as my butt got cold on those hard, cold floors during meditation, or I got whacked with a stick by the Head Monk for nodding off, I would be out of there. It may work for some, but that is not my style. Not that it wouldn't be a cool experience. It's just that I am more valuable in another role of which I chose; an unconventional one; a spiritual butt kicker. It is a style of teaching that works for some and I know that you are either well on your way to awakening (which is why you are reading this) or you understand why you are here at this critical time on our planet. Awakening is not one place. It is a frequency of which has no end to its expansion. Awakening leads to enlightenment that leads to more exploration, more roles, more contrast and higher realms to reach. Awakening is simply waking up to this, letting go of anything else and nothing more. Awakening is a return to consciousness.

Whom should you listen to when it comes to spiritual teachings? So many spiritual teachers seem to have conflicting opinions. It can be confusing. Who should you believe? Who has the answers? Everyone does. If one believes something, then it is true for them. It is that simple. The One likes variety. Your indicator that a teacher is coming from a higher frequency begins with empowering you, and second, they will never preach fear. That subject is reserved for those still entrenched in the matrix game on the material level. My mission is to share the message that we are powerful beings, ready to awaken and to love ourselves and others once again. It feels good to do that, doesn't it? That is because we are knowing our origins and that always feels 'right.' Always go with your intuition no matter how popular another's message is. What you believe today may not be your truth next year or even next week. You should honor your own personal evolution and know that there are no mistakes. The One doesn't make mistakes and neither can you.

We are not required to behave a certain way to know that we are awakened. We can drink coffee, have a glass of wine, and maybe even curse once in a while. It is possible that you are awakened and don't know it. Awakening is not placing rules on others or the planet, dictating a certain way of living, or beliefs. Awakening is total acceptance and the realization that being human is amazing, and challenging, and difficult, and the ultimate school. It is being aware of your existence and making the best possible choices in each moment. It is giving compassion over judgement, giving over greed, and unconditional love. It is service to others and knowing that it's okay to take care of you too!

Even the Dalai Lama on occasion responds with "I don't know" when asked about how the universe works and other deep questions. No human has all of the answers. We aren't supposed to. We did not imagine how difficult the journey could be because we, in our purest form, could not know the depths of pain that humans have conjured. Of course, that is, until we get here. Welcome to the master class.

THE GREAT AWAKENING

The 'great' awakening is simply a greater percentage of the matrix players shifting into a higher, more powerful frequency, closer to connection to Oneness. It is that tipping point I spoke of, but is the 'tip' toward love. Simply put it is the recognition that our experience as humans is a self-created illusion and that we are the creators behind it all. The majority of humans will not achieve this state of being. This is not necessary to transform the planet as the influence of light has a much more powerful affect than darkness. One cannot darken a room full of light without extinguishing it. A dark room can, however, transform into light even with a match. This raises the frequency on our planet and creates a tipping point in the matrix program from a dense to a more expansive and caring one. This higher frequency brings us closer to unity and oneness, which is service to others. From this space, we will change the future of our planet and all of its inhabitants.

Each awakening affects the collective. This is the only way it can be, because all beings including dense beings will feel this great lightness, compassion and love. Awakened beings will not see others as enemies or take sides. There will be no reason for conflict because they will know that the other is themselves and all things. They will see the light in others, extend their support and acceptance. Enlightened humans do not see the fault in the other, but the pain and fear that drives their actions. This is compassion. Those still operating in density will find themselves prompted to make different, higher choices. It does not, however, promise total freedom from the challenges here. They will still exist but are perceived differently because we will see them as beautiful opportunities to express all of the gifts we hold and share them. After all, this is the game. Otherwise we would simply dissolve our human form and go back into purity. There is a heaven on earth that can exist. A great awakening means that there are no real endings, no lack, nothing to fear. We will embrace the challenges and truly understand their beauty. From here, a new world blooms wherein we focus on solutions, community, creativity and sharing. This can happen in your lifetime and certainly within your own reality.

AS THE WORLD AWAKENS, THE EGO WILL BATTLE FOR CONTROL

As humans awaken to their origin of perfection that will end suffering, the frequency of the collective planet will raise. This is the culmination of the 'cycle' of being human and progression to the next stage of 'knowing.' We now know suffering, limitations and fear. What is next for this dense species? A form that exists in the illusion of limitations that no longer believes this. It now expands outside of the confines of the matrix, celebrating the return to consciousness. This is what we refer to as 'the great awakening.' In this state, we KNOW what we are, ACCEPT why we are here, and KNOW how powerful and meaningful it all is, challenges and all! We are awakening to and KNOW that what we are experiencing is the illusion created by us that provides this unfamiliar, uncomfortable journey. How very simple it all becomes! We KNOW that we are not these separate bodies but One cohesive energy living out an adventure together; each affecting the other and participating as the One. We are coming into consciousness to know that as we serve others, we serve ourselves. As we serve ourselves, we serve others. There is no dividing line. Even the ugly ego is the creator knowing its unconscious form. The awakened one is looking at his/her self when it sees the ego. They are one in the same.

This shift to service to others will take us into a more cooperative and balanced community. It will generate positivity, giving, caring, respect, hope and compassion that will be felt by all humans, animals and nature. This is a direct threat to the ego that places its needs first. Those clinging to the material world and service to self will battle to maintain their perceived power and control. Those who fear loss in any form will take sides to preserve the old way of life. The ego will fear and feel lack, fear change, will hoard to preserve itself, blame others, and respond with anger. Aggressive behavior will be demonstrated and fear-based media, false stories, and influences to cause separation will accelerate.

Enlightened ones must be on guard. Awakening is not a place you maintain without effort. The influences of the collective can change any situation because each of us has free will. Therefore, those choosing light will need to remain steadfast in compassion, love, and serving others. They will truly be tested as the ego-driven population pushes its separation agenda, claiming that there is a battle taking place where there actually is none. Awakened humans not fully enlightened may be tempted to 'take a side' on behalf of the good for all. However, taking a 'side' is not awakening. It is still separation no matter what cause one fights for. The solution to this is creation of new ways that are inclusive and expansive. Dissolving structures that have never truly worked in favor of the whole must be replaced with new systems. This must be the focus of awakened beings, acting on behalf of all but not imposing it.

This is the final cycle of the great density game on planet earth, of course until another begins. Will the seemingly 'easy' path of clinging to the material comforts win? It will never satisfy as we have learned and is an endless game. Will we recognize that we are indestructible and that there are no real endings? Will we embrace what lies beyond this human existence that offers the abundance, love and euphoria that we continually strive to capture on earth?

The creator is in continuous expansion. The ego believes there is a 'place and time' where happiness resides. The quest for this in the material world is never found because joy lies in a much deeper, simpler place that each of us already carry. It is not something someone may 'get' nor 'get to.' Whatever it gains, it never feels satisfaction and continues to search. This is because true joy does not lie in density. This creates an endless cycle of extremes of short-term happiness and dissatisfaction.

Imagine the ego believing that what it 'knows' and is familiar with is moving further away and possibly dissolving, even if that familiarity is something that it has never quite achieved. This certainly prompts pure fear. The thought of Oneness is its enemy. Sharing is what it does only to obtain 'something' that it benefits from including recognition or a sense of importance. In the face of what it perceives is crisis, its only option is to battle for preservation of its world. Losing this is the equivalent to death. Ironically the death of the ego is the very thing that will open the gateways to that true happiness. The ego does not give up easily.

There are those who will not accept the transition into Oneness. They do not believe in that which lies outside of its logical world. It is incomprehensible nonsense to them. Therefore, they may never transition into light on their journey here. This is not the end, of course. It is simply a choice not to fully participate in the ultimate transition that this matrix challenge offers. Some may exit early, unwilling to continue this difficult task. There are always options to complete their chosen assignments. It may take the form in another illusion on another planet or another dimension. Because we have the privilege of free will, we are not obligated to awaken here. There is no judgement about this decision. Some may truly enjoy the conflict and controversy. It may bring joy and fascination that the person is not willing to give up. They choose to not contribute to the collective transition of the planet. This will take them to another learning experience in another illusion.

When we state that 'the meek shall inherit the earth' we speak of those who do not 'fight' for rights or use conflict for gain. They hold powers that do not require physical force. Their presence affects their surroundings and the reactions of those near and far. The meek need nothing. They battle for nothing. Therefore, there is no resistance to the egos that seek control. The meek are changemakers who focus on positive creations that include even those whom pose as their worst enemies. They will not fight, but the meek are not weak and submissive. They are strong in their powers that will always place the concerns of others first. Their victories are won in inclusion, compassion and love. No one is a threat. The 'other' is an aspect of all creation and they view all as equal. They are willing to take a back seat, requiring no accolades or recognition for their efforts.

The ego is on the opposite spectrum to the meek. It sees everyone as a threat except those that provide what it desires. It is cynical and self-serving. It is the lowest frequency and has strong attachments. It must be heard, is loud and boastful, controlling, and will battle in the name of its 'just' cause. It preys on other egos that live in fear and can be very persuasive. It is capable of doing great damage and keeps the matrix in a lower form of operation. Anything lower has destroyed itself only to hurl back into a new journey. None of this is 'wrong' or 'bad' except according to humans who label it that way. It simply 'is.' Like everything, it is experience and 'knowing' that which it can be. Who are we to condemn that 'other' part of us?

For every breakup, there is often a party claiming that the other is a narcissist. Have you heard anyone use that term? The finger pointing is rampant. Perhaps we are confusing narcissistic behavior with the ego. In that case, all of the world is narcissistic. Which brings us to the one labeling the other. It seems that those coming out of breakups never contributed toward the demise of the relationship, according to their story. Therefore, one has to wonder if the offending party suddenly became a narcissist, or were they always that way? If always, then didn't the partner pointing the finger opt into that relationship? They certainly must have been attracted to such behavior. Here is the official definition according to the Mayo Clinic . . .

"Narcissistic personality disorder is a mental health condition in which people have an unreasonably high sense of their own importance. They need and seek too much attention and want people to admire them. People with this disorder may lack the ability to understand or care about the feelings of others.

Narcissistic personality disorder involves a pattern of self-centered, arrogant thinking and behavior, a lack of empathy and consideration for other people, and an excessive need for admiration. Others often describe people with NPD as cocky, manipulative, selfish, patronizing, and demanding."

Don't most humans seek attention and approval, lack empathy for others and have a tendency to manipulate and demand? Don't we all operate on some level of narcissistic behavior? An even bigger question is "what is considered normal behavior?" At what point does it become excessive that warrants such a label? It was acceptable to many going into relationships but when the ego is not satisfied, the offending party is now the enemy and labeled abnormal. What does that actually mean?

What part of you operates within ego and what operates on the level of narcissist? Isn't labeling the other, deflecting responsibility, and announcing that someone has somehow harmed you an aspect of arrogance and sense of self-importance? These labels are ALL indications of ego in action. The varying levels of offense are irrelevant. It is all finger pointing as soon as ego's needs or desires are not fulfilled. Who, what, and when, or details of the situation does not matter. Whenever blame is deflected, you can bet that the ego is in charge. It sees narcissistic behavior as an offense, but somehow ignores the judgement and blame it dishes out about that person. Is that not also self-importance and lack of compassion? The whole discussion and labeling is more of ego separating us into 'right' and 'wrong' according to its own rules. This behavior continues the vicious cycle of ego battling to be right. At what point do we start looking at ourselves and end the hypocrisy?

Our current challenges have prompted many to seek unconventional means of escaping the pain of the material world, such as spiritual paths. My thoughts are that this will accelerate as the tipping point is giving us the 'in your face' reality of what we have done to ourselves and our planet. This unconventional path of awakening is unknown to humans. It isn't like running a race and then deciding to run a marathon. We know what it is to walk and run. Awakening, we do not know. It is a mysterious journey of which the path is new to every seeker, with no clear directions. The ego, of course, wants clarity. It wants to know 'how' one can get there, what to expect, what results will it produce. Awakening cannot be achieved with the thinking mind. The mind sets out to solve its problem of unhappiness with logical steps. One cannot reach enlightenment with thoughts and a set of instructions. The death of the ego must take place, although not entirely. It can serve its purpose in survival situations and is part of the matrix attributes. Perhaps it is clearer to state that the ego must 'step aside' in order to open the gateway to enlightenment.

We are like infants. To be a child is a continual growing and learning process. It includes skinned knees, sometimes broken bones or worse. It includes hurting others, being harmed, along with learning how to function independently. Being a child simply 'is' our growth process. No one escapes this. It is necessary. One cannot 'awaken' if one was never ignorant. We must know ignorance to achieve awakening. Is being a baby wrong? Experiencing the state of ego is no more wrong than being that ignorant, helpless baby.

Like the baby who does not know what is good for it, the ego simply 'wants.' When it does not receive those wants, it cries and often throws a fit. It cannot know what is best for it. So, it learns. However, babies do not have the conscious capacity to blow up the planet. Herein is where we see the ego as much more dangerous than an evolving spirit. The ego that has no interest in escaping the pain of the material world but continues to battle for it will not give up easily.

Be prepared. The baby that is not getting what it wants will kick and scream in ways we have never seen before. It doesn't understand that there is another way, another choice. It cannot be faulted for this lack of experience or knowledge. It is not even capable of such thoughts as its reactions are based purely on a material world and its needs within it. How can we get angry at a crawling baby for not knowing how to run! It is insane to want that, yet that is exactly how we respond to dense humans. Ironically, wanting THEM to be different and more advanced is OUR ego not accepting another's condition or choice. It is an ongoing battle that never resolves itself. Full awareness is necessary on the part of the awakened. It includes acceptance and non-judgment of those 'others' we feel are the problem in our world. When we offer a 'better' option, we can appeal to the egos that want to be a part of something that brings joy in the physical world. If it fulfills their desires, they will feel complete if even for a moment in time. And that is OK. Even Mother Teresa accepted money from drug kings. She said their money purchased goods just as well as from anyone else. Who is to say if the 'anyone else' was any more caring or sincere than the drug dealer? This is why judgement can work against us as we seek to evolve. We must focus on solutions. They will shine the light on a new pathway that others are not positioned to find. We must be the leaders of positive change that can close the gap between us all.

The battle for control is the ego's self-inflicted war. When the awakened do not engage, there is no war. Herein the meek shall inherit the earth.

THE KNOWING

There is a state of being I call 'the knowing.' It is a state of wonderment and peace, even in the midst of human chaos. It is beyond the ego and has no labels, explanations, questions or answers. It is where one 'knows' that all is purposeful but not in the way humans think. It is a much higher understanding not comprehensible by egos. How and why we exist is not important. The 'knowing' is the release of the human requirement to have answers to anything. The desire for answers dissolves. ALL simply IS and from this place there is peace. The ALL that is happening is Source experiencing and exploring. This process is eternal. Creation has no limitation.

Are you ready to go into the KNOWING? It is full acceptance without questions. It requires nothing. It has power beyond what we access as dense humans and takes us into realms where we can fly. It is the expansion of your energy consciousness into all that is. It is accepting your human experience but knowing that it is an adventure and that YOU are that and everything else. It accepts this role and plays it out beautifully, as you intended when you chose it. All you have to do is to embrace this illusion and go into awareness and positive, conscious response within each moment. Release the ego's requirement to have answers to that which it cannot comprehend and KNOW that all is well and will be revealed in divine time.

Where do we go from here? Anywhere you desire. You cannot make a mistake. This is your story that you are writing, acting in and only you determine the ending. It is one play in the many you will choose and participate in. As 'real' as this illusion appears to be, it expands far beyond your role here and your choices hold so much more importance than you may believe. The human unconscious state protects our dense brains from the mind-blowing, overwhelming information that exists outside of our illusion and how things really work. It also obscures our awareness of that expansive power that is always in use, but due to our unconscious, self-limited state, is not directed in the highest manner.

I assure you that as uncomfortable as it may seem to let go of that world that you 'think' you know, what awaits beyond will amaze you in ways that humans cannot comprehend. Letting go is required. What you hold onto that defines, labels, and judges, limits you. These are the veils that must be removed in order to see clearly. That's it. Nothing more or less. Can you do it? Of course, you can. You must simply stop believing the stories that your ego, your programmed past, and society tells you. End the analysis, the thinking, the blame, and the control that isn't working for you. The addiction to the pursuit of happiness wears thin and can tailspin you into the abyss of anxiety and depression. Where is the happiness? It is fleeting when you live on the ego's terms. You may find that the ego that clings to the material world for satisfaction is not as difficult to let go as you may have thought because it has proven that it does not perform or produce results in the manner we desire. The returns for releasing this vicious cycle of manifesting from the ego's directives will be enormous and satisfying in ways that the illusion cannot provide. True happiness, in its pure form that is consistent, is found in a space where it has no conditions. It relies on nothing, therefore there are no other factors that can remove you from it. It is a state of being of which you can achieve if you end your reliance on ego and its false promises.

You may not know where to start and want answers NOW. Your ego-controlled mind will want 'steps' or 'techniques' to get results as fast as possible. It wants a clear path from here to there because it believes in tangible and understandable ways to receive results. I have them for you, but it does not come with a push button formula that relies on physical actions such as mantras or vision boards. Ego wants the magical words to open the vault. What opens the vault is not words but beliefs and frequencies. That entails a much deeper look into what yours are.

Breaking through fear releases the blame and forgiveness pattern. Years of therapy are not needed when you have an understanding of your powers, because analysis makes no sense in a world where pain and challenges have positive purpose. You are never a victim and your life will make sense. In fact, the more challenges that you have taken on, the more you will realize that you are a major warrior in this matrix game. Your opportunities are enormous!

Are you ready to get started? It won't be painful, and it could liberate you in ways never imagined. My question is, 'what is the alternative?' There is a 'beyond' that is so beautiful that you have known. It is within you now. It awaits your discovery and you can access it in your lifetime. Bliss is a state of being that you choose. What will you choose?

ABOUT THE AUTHOR

Landria Onkka is a best-selling, award winning author. Her book "The Rooftop Christmas Tree" was made into a Hallmark Movie and can be viewed on Amazon Prime. She is an influencer and teaches students worldwide how to 'break through fear.' Her online courses have received five stars and consistent, amazing results.

You can find her courses at https://landriaonkka.com **and can follow Landria on her YouTube channel** https://www.youtube.com/c/landriaonkka

Receive free inspirational videos to your email at https://landriaonkka.com/free-inspiration **and follow her on Instagram** https://www.instagram.com/landriaonkkateachings/